JUDAH P. BENJAMIN

His Escape to England Through Florida

RICHARD A. SANCHEZ

Contents

"I intend to go to the farthest place from the United States…if it takes me to the middle of China."

Judah P. Benjamin,
Abbeville SC, 1865

Judah P. Benjamin
In Florida

Introduction

The inspiration to embark on this research project came from my interest in the life of Frederick Tresca, the lighthouse keeper on Egmont Key, Florida, from 1856 to 1858. His story became intertwined with Judah P. Benjamin, the Confederate Secretary of State, and his escape through the South from Richmond to Bimini and eventually to Great Britain. Tresca and Benjamin became acquainted when he was planning to leave Florida by boat near Sarasota, Florida, in June of 1865. Before arriving in Florida, he had spent the previous months traveling in various disguises from Richmond through the Confederate States. Judah Benjamin spent two weeks at Tresca's home just south of the village of Manatee (present-day Bradenton) after nearly being captured by Union forces at the Gamble Plantation several miles away. Tresca and Benjamin traveled together for the following weeks, putting in many days sailing the Gulf Coast of Florida to Knight's Key and eventually to Bimini in the Bahamas, then Nassau. He arrived in Southampton, England, and safety after months of hazard-filled travel.

Many books have been written over the years about the fall of the Confederacy and the attempted escape of President Jefferson Davis and others in the government. Several books have been written about Judah Benjamin and his life, political views, and legal career before the Civil War. One book, *"Judah P. Benjamin — Statesman of the Lost Cause,"* was printed in 1933, many decades before the Internet, and others have been written by authors who didn't live in or visit Florida for research. Most accounts agree on the events until Davis's capture near Irwinville, Georgia, in 1865. After that, I found incorrect information, conflicting accounts, and a lack of information altogether. So, I intend to fill in the gaps with this book and correct the stories about his time in Florida.

Now, with so many documents and records online at the fingertips of researchers, details of Judah Benjamin's journey through Florida can be filled in and fact-checked with much more accuracy. Also, county historical societies and local museums are excellent resources for historical details in each location. Since I live in the state, it is relatively easy for me to visit each of the sites and towns mentioned in the publications and see for myself if the narratives correlate. I endeavored to visit as many locations as possible mentioned in the narratives, which was made more difficult due to COVID-19 restrictions on libraries and museums. Also, with the availability of satellite imagery with Google Earth, I can quickly get an eagle's eye view of a location and visit out-of-state sites. I could view Pere Lachaise Cemetery in Paris from above to get a sense of the size of this final resting place of Judah Benjamin.

One of the problems with researching an elusive figure like Judah Benjamin was his obsession with secrecy about his life. His documents about his time in the Confederate government were burned upon his departure from Richmond, Virginia, in April of 1865. His papers about his time in England and Paris were also destroyed upon his death in 1884. He kept no journal or diary, and no correspondence books have survived. He didn't talk publicly about his experiences after the war. Speaking with author Francis Lawley in 1883, near the end of his life, Benjamin said

> "Even if I had health and desired ever so much to help you in your work, I have no materials available for your purpose. I have never kept a diary or retained a copy of a letter written by me. No letters addressed to me by others will be found among my papers when I die. With perhaps the exception of Mrs. Jefferson Davis, no one has many letters of mine, for I have read so many American biographies that reflect only the passions and prejudices of their writers that I do not want to leave behind my letters and documents to be used in such a work about myself."

So, the complete story of his time in Florida and beyond will always have some mysteries that will never be solved. In the case of two different narratives about an event, I worked to determine which was the most likely under the circumstances. Still, I presented the alternative and explained why I chose one. So, I hope you find this book interesting and enjoyable to read. Hopefully, you will read some of the earlier works on Judah Benjamin written by others.

Chapter One

Judah Benjamin
Before the War

Many books have been written on the life and politics of Judah Philip Benjamin. He was a great legal mind, author, planter, experimenter, orator, politician, and businessman among his many accomplishments. But the quote from Winston Churchill about Russia, "a riddle, wrapped inside a mystery, inside an enigma," would also apply to Judah Benjamin. He kept no journals, diaries, or letters of his life. Letters sent to siblings were destroyed on his request, with only a few writings by others surviving to give a hint about who he was. I think he would be more well-known and appreciated if not for his prominent roles in the government of the Confederacy during the Civil War, his position on slavery, and his ownership of enslaved people before the war. I don't want to rehash the more detailed works of others about his life. Still, I think it's necessary to recap his story so that the significance of his passing through Florida during his escape after the war's end can be appreciated.

Judah Benjamin was born the third of nine[1] children on August 6, 1811, in the port town of Christiansted, on the island of St Croix in the Danish West Indies (now the US Virgin Islands). He was named after a sibling who had died in infancy. At the time of his birth, St. Croix was a British possession. It would be occupied by the British from 1801 to 1802 and again from 1807 to 1815 because of the Napoleonic Wars. Being born during the British occupation would be crucial to his safe passage out of the United States many decades later and would allow him to claim British citizenship. His parents were Philip Benjamin and former Rebecca de Mendes. They were Sephardic Jews whose ancestors had emigrated from the Iberian Peninsula to London.

The Benjamin family included two enslaved people who were domestic helpers. Undoubtedly, this fact influenced Judah's attitude towards slavery in general and personally enslaving people many years later. For young Judah, enslaving people was a regular part of his life, even after moving to the United States.

At a young age, his family emigrated to the United States and settled in Wilmington, North Carolina, becoming merchants. His uncle Jacob Levy was also a merchant in Wilmington and had encouraged the Benjamins to settle there. In 1817, Jacob Levy purchased some land near Fayetteville, and the Benjamin family also moved to be near him. Judah began attending the prestigious Fayetteville Academy, with Jacob paying for his tuition along with Judah's brother Solomon and sister Hannah. He studied under the tutelage of Reverend Colin McIver.

Jacob Levy suffered a business failure, and he and the Benjamins moved in 1822 to Charleston, South Carolina, to seek their fortunes

---

1 Judah's siblings were Solomon, Harriet Hannah Mendes, Peninah, Jacob Levy Benjamin, Rebecca Levy, Judith, Joseph, and Moses.

there. Charleston had the largest Jewish population in the United States at the time and was tolerant of different religions. It also had a large slave population. The family moved to the city at a time of rising tensions between the enslaved people and slaveholders.

Charleston had more enslaved people than whites at the time, and rumors were swirling about a pending slave revolt led by an enslaved person, Denmark Vesey. There was talk of enslaved people murdering the men, raping the women, and burning the town and port. In the end, the revolt was stopped before any of the threats were carried out, but not before many enslaved people, whether participating in the revolt or not, had been publicly hanged, sometimes dozens at once. The locals took to hiding their slaves lest they be implicated in the uprising and be summarily hanged as well. Undoubtedly, this impacted Judah and his attitudes towards the treatment of enslaved people in later years.

The principal of the Fayetteville Academy at that time was Reverend Dr. Dyer Ball, who recognized Judah's intelligence very quickly. Dr. Ball had connections with the faculty of Yale College (now Yale University) in Connecticut. Since Judah's parents could not pay for his attendance, Dr. Ball arranged for his admission with Benjamin's promise of paying back tuition to the college when he became established in a career.

In 1825, at age fourteen, Benjamin began his studies at Yale College. He was initially well-received by the other students due to his young age. They loaned or gave him money to help him with daily expenses. However, they soon noticed that they began missing articles from their rooms and, before long, realized that Judah was the perpetrator. But they overlooked his transgressions and initially didn't report his thefts. Soon, a significant sum of money went missing from one of the classmates' rooms, and Judah was taken before the faculty to answer the charges. Later, upon searching Judah's room and trunk, they found many penknives, pencil cases, and other small articles.

Judah resigned in 1827, and his fellow students decided to give him some money so he could travel. They advised him to leave the city before the matter was turned over to civil authorities. Thus, his college career ended when he was sixteen without earning a degree. When Dr. Ball was later informed of the events, he commented that he had been aware of Judah's tendencies and was dismayed since he thought he had cured him of the habit of petty theft. Unfortunately, Judah would continue with these transgressions in his following location.

Judah still hoped that he could someday return to Yale College. He wrote a letter to the President, Reverend Jeremiah Day, in January of 1828, which read in part:

> Rev. Jeremiah Day:
> Highly Respected Sir:
>
> It is with shame and diffidence that I now address you to solicit your forgiveness and interference with the Faculty in my behalf. And I beseech you, Sir, not to attribute my improper conduct to any design or intentional violation of the laws of the college, nor to suppose that I would be guilty of any premeditated disrespect to yourself or any member of the faculty...

After signing it as J. P. Benjamin, he added a postscript: "May I solicit, Sir (if not too troublesome to you) the favor of a few lines in answer to this letter, that I may be able to judge the possibility of my return to the University?"

However, it was not to be, and soon Judah was on his way to the next chapter of his life. Unfortunately, these youthful infractions at Yale would follow him for the rest of his time in the United States, being brought up by his detractors on several occasions.

After leaving Connecticut and heading for Albany, New York, Benjamin met Col. Samuel Stone of Rochester. Benjamin had told him of his situation and that he was destitute. Stone was sympathetic to his plight, gave him money, and suggested he accompany him to Rochester to find employment as a teacher at Brayton's High School. Mr. Brayton, the school's owner and a merchant, found him a place to live at a boarding house operated by Mrs. Leonard, a widow, and provided him with suitable clothing from his store. Benjamin worked at the school for nine months and then disappeared, departing town without notice, leaving unpaid bills at the boarding house and debts to Mr. Stone.

Soon after this experience in Rochester, he moved to New Orleans, Louisiana, and began working first in a mercantile house, but only for a few months. Judah later commented that his time at the mercantile house was a valuable experience for his law career. He later secured work as a law clerk by Mr. Greenbury R. Stringer. A local notary, Stringer, agreed to teach him the law in the evenings after work. Benjamin gained practical experience in legal forms and procedures while working for Stringer.

New Orleans was a booming port town that brought goods from around the world to be distributed via the Mississippi River to the interior of the US. It was also how goods from the country's interior were exported abroad. The city played an essential part in the Atlantic slave trade during the antebellum period.

New Orleans had a large and diverse population, including wealthy Creoles. Benjamin earned extra money by teaching local Creole ladies English.

Benjamin townhouse at 327 Bourbon Street is now undergoing renovations. Judah and Natalie lived on the second floor.

One day, a wealthy planter contacted Mr. Stringer and asked if he could recommend a tutor to teach his daughter English. Stringer suggested Judah, but after meeting him, the planter said he thought him unsuitable for the job. Judah was not unqualified, but he was so charming and entertaining that he believed his daughter would fall in love with him. The planter was Auguste St. Martin, and his daughter was Natalie.

Despite the father's reservations, Judah was hired as Natalie's tutor. Judah realized the necessity of being fluent in French, so Natalie taught him Creole French in exchange for him teaching her English.

Auguste's fears were realized soon after the classes began. Judah fell hopelessly in love with her, almost "love at first sight." The St. Martins were a prominent local family, and Judah and Natalie eventually began a courtship that led to marriage.

Judah and Natalie were married on February 12, 1833. At least that's when the Notary Public signed the marriage contract. Mr. Stringer was one of the witnesses for the groom. The contract came with a dowry. It listed the mulatto girl *Mary, age about sixteen, estimee' dix Cents piastres; the mulatto girl Martha, about twelve, estimee' quatre Cent piastres.* The marriage was not a happy one since Natalie was not a traditional wife but had a bit of a wild streak. She could not be faithful to one man and engaged in infidelities. Benjamin, despite this, vowed to love her always. The couple lived in Natalie's parents' home at 327 Bourbon Street for the first three years of their marriage until Judah could afford to move into their own place.

In 1837, ten years after Benjamin left Rochester, his old acquaintance, Col. Stone, was in New Orleans for business, where Benjamin was now practicing law. Col. Stone was staying at the Saint Charles Hotel, looked across the street, and saw a sign that read "J. P. Benjamin Attorney at Law," wondering if it may be the same Judah

Benjamin that had stiffed him years before. He remembered the amount he was owed and added ten years' worth of interest, wrote a bill, and then walked across the street to find out if it was the same person. When he walked into the office, he asked if he was J. P. Benjamin, and when the answer was "yes," Col Stone said, "I am Col. Sam Stone, from Rochester, New York, and I want the money on this bill." Benjamin looked at Stone and then the bill and, without a word, reached into his pocket, took out the money, and paid the amount. He never asked about Widow Leonard or anything about Rochester. Col. Stone stayed at the hotel for a month but never spoke to Benjamin again after that encounter.

Belle Chase Plantation was demolished in the 1960s

With his thriving law practice, Benjamin soon had enough money to purchase a sugar plantation. The existing house was found to be unsuitable for his family, so he demolished that house and built a much larger and grander home he called "Belle Chasse." It was in Plaquemines Parrish along the Mississippi River. The new house was constructed for $28,000 (nearly a million dollars today). He learned to be a sugar cane grower and eventually owned one hundred forty enslaved people there. He took on a partner in this enterprise, Theodore Packwood. Cultivating sugar cane was a new industry in Louisiana at that time. Refining cane was somewhat primitive and labor intensive, with a lot of waste and inefficient boiling of the cane in a series of open vats called a "Jamaican train."

He was always the innovator and conducted experiments in refining sugar cane to make a better product. His experiments were an attempt to improve the process and yielded some successes in both the quantity and quality of the molasses. He hired Norbert Rillieux[2] to construct his revolutionary evaporation system at Belle Chasse. He became a staunch supporter of Rillieux among the planters of Louisiana. Benjamin said the sugar he produced with the Rillieux evaporator equals "the best double-refined sugar of our northern refineries."

He had built a grand two-story home to please Natalie, but she soon tired of the plantation life, and after a few months living there, she left for Paris, leaving only a short note telling Benjamin. Natalie was pregnant then and was determined that her child would not be raised on a plantation so far from civilization. She gave birth to Julie

---

2 Norbert Rillieux (1806-1894), a free man of color, was a chemist and engineer born in New Orleans who developed a process and evaporator for refining raw sugar cane into sugar. The method produced a higher quality product, more efficiently and with less energy needed in the process.

Marie Natalie Benjamin in 1843 and was called "Ninette." Judah was resigned to visiting her once a year until near the end of his life in Paris. Judah soon lost interest in being a plantation owner and turned the operation over to his business partner, Theodore Packwood.

Judah Benjamin became a successful and busy lawyer in New Orleans, winning many of his cases. His career and reputation were boosted by publishing a book titled *"Digest of the Reported Decisions of the Superior Court of the Late Territory of Orleans and the Supreme Court of the State of Louisiana."* He was only twenty-three at the time of its publication! The book was co-authored with Thomas Slidell, a former classmate at Yale. His brother John Slidell would later become the Confederate diplomat to France during the Civil War.

One of the most controversial cases, considering his personal views of slavery, was one where twenty enslaved people had been transported to Nassau in the Bahamas. The enslaved people had taken control of the brig *Creole* on the high seas, killed the slaveowner's agent, wounded the captain, and then sailed into port. Some of the enslaved people had gone ashore. There, the enslaved people were considered freed since Great Britain had abolished slavery. The original owners filed a suit to have them returned, but Benjamin argued successfully at trial that they should remain free. This became an international incident and nearly caused military action by the British against the United States.

Judah was a workaholic by any standard, but he did like to get away from New Orleans and have some leisure time. When his caseload was lighter in the summers, he would travel to Beaufort to visit with family and spend many hours fishing for "devil fish." This type of devil ray or manta ray was abundant in nearby Port Royal Sound. He would use a harpoon and, after successfully spearing one, would fight to bring it to shore. He was often accompanied by a companion named Hannibal, possibly an enslaved person.

Benjamin became involved in business ventures concerning railroad construction, one project as a legal adviser and promoter of a rail line between Jackson, Mississippi, and New Orleans, completed in 1858. It significantly sped up the shipment of cotton for planters around New Orleans. Once a part of the Illinois-Central Line, it is now an essential part of the Canadian National Railway, being purchased in 1988.

He briefly participated in a business venture to build a railroad across the Mexican Isthmus of Tehuantepec to have a shorter and faster route from New Orleans to California. The Tehuantepec Company was formed, and survey work was done on the proposed route. But the venture ended for good before any work had started due to shipping delays causing cost increases, outbreaks of yellow fever, inaction by both Mexican and American officials, and the outbreak of the Civil War. Benjamin stepped away from all his railroading activities as his interest in politics grew.

Benjamin soon entered local politics as a Whig and was elected to the Louisiana House of Representatives. He advocated for free public schools for both boys and girls where they should be given a primary education and instruction in the principles of government so students could "discriminate between the artful demagogue and the shallow pretender, and the man whose true merits should inspire their confidence and respect."

Benjamin was instrumental in drafting the Louisiana Constitution of 1845. It replaced the one from 1812, which restricted voting only to landowners that favored Whigs. The new one kept that provision and added free white men to eligible voters. It did not allow active military soldiers to vote. The new constitution added public schools as well.

He became involved in national politics when President Franklin Pierce offered him a nomination to the US Supreme Court. Benjamin declined since it would interfere with his thriving and lucrative law practice. In addition, he was elected as a United States Senator in 1853 as a Whig to represent Louisiana.

He was not the first Jew to hold such a high elected office. David Levy Yulee, a fellow Sephardic Jew from Florida, had preceded Benjamin to Congress by a few years. As a senator, Benjamin became an ardent spokesman for slavery, many times delivering eloquent speeches in the Senate in favor of it.

He eventually changed parties from the Whig to the Democrat party in May 1856. At this time, in 1858, he became friends with Jefferson Davis and his wife, Varina. Davis was the Secretary of War but would soon be elected US Senator of Mississippi. Davis and Benjamin were ambitious politicians, and the friendship was described as "wary." That would change in due time with secession.

There is an account of an incident in 1858 where a verbal clash occurred between the two men on the floor of the Senate over a $100,000 appropriation for the purchase of breech-loading rifles for the Army. Benjamin questioned Davis on where the funding was coming from, either from an appropriation or the Treasury. Benjamin accused Davis of giving "a sneering reply to what was certainly a very respectful inquiry." Davis countered, "I consider it an attempt to misrepresent a very plain remark." The exchange continued until Davis was angered and commented about having to argue with a paid attorney. The dispute ended when Davis publicly apologized to Benjamin in the Senate, stating, "I have been wholly wrong." This incident revealed much about the two men's personalities but did not negatively affect their working relationship.

The Decatur House

During his time in Washington, Benjamin stayed at the Decatur House[3]. It had been the rental home of many prominent tenants since the death of its owner, John Gatsby. It was a three-story Federal-style brick structure that included slave quarters.

Natalie and Ninette had been living in Paris, and Benjamin would visit them annually in the summer when his workload was less. He had hoped to woo her back to Washington, DC, to live with

---

3   The Decatur House was built in 1818 by naval hero Stephen Decatur. It is located at 748 Jackson Place in Washington, DC. An outbuilding was added in 1836, which included quarters for enslaved people. After a series of owners, it was used as a rental until the Civil War, and Judah Benjamin was the last tenant. Since 2010, the Decatur House has been a museum and houses the National Center for White House History.

him. 1858, after his reelection to the Senate, he implemented a plan to entice her back. He extensively redecorated the house with the finest paintings, china, crystal, and silver. Local society ladies were informed, and he hired servants with experience in giving large formal parties.

Benjamin worshipped Natalie and was willing to do anything to please her. It was to no avail. The local society ladies snubbed her, and Natalie showed no interest in them. She engaged in numerous affairs and was not very discreet about them.

Finally, in 1859, Natalie decided to return to Paris. Benjamin auctioned all the finery he had purchased for Natalie, but he couldn't bear to be present when people came to view items for sale. Natalie had caused her husband great embarrassment and emotional stress, and he was glad to see her leave Washington for Paris. They continued to see each other once a year in Paris, even though it meant separation from Ninette, who was sixteen then. He trusted Natalie to raise her properly in his absence.

Chapter Two

Secession and the War Years

T he contentious issue of slavery led to threats from Southern states to leave the Union to form the Confederate States of America. Judah Benjamin favored secession, but only as a last resort. He was part of a group of moderate Southerners who wanted to preserve the Union but, in the end, were unable to compromise on the issue of slavery. Slavery was such a vital part of the South, both economically and socially, that ending it outright was not an option as some abolitionists advocated.

Many people in the South believed that a war would likely not last very long, so the possibility of war was of little concern. Benjamin realized that the Southern states' seceding would eventually lead to a costly war with an uncertain outcome. Louisiana seceded on January 26, 1861, after a vote of 113 for and 17 against secession, the sixth state to do so. He and his Louisiana colleague, John Slidell, resigned from the US Senate on February 4, 1861, nine days after their state voted to secede from the Union. Judah left Washington shortly after resigning since he feared arrest as a rebel and promptly returned to New Orleans.

Jefferson Davis

Eventually, eleven Southern states left the Union to form the Confederacy. Maryland might have sided with the Confederacy, but the Union Army quickly occupied the state due to its proximity to Washington.

Benjamin was soon called into service of the fledgling nation by his friend, Jefferson Davis, who was now Provisional President of the new country. He was elected unanimously by delegates from the Constitutional Convention in Montgomery, Alabama. Davis took office on February 18, 1861. Davis needed an Attorney General for the new country and could think of no one more qualified than Judah Benjamin. In Davis's memoirs, he remarked that Benjamin "had a very high reputation as a lawyer, and my acquaintance with him in the Senate impressed me with the lucidity of his intellect, systematic habits, and capacity for labor." Judah readily accepted the post on February 26 but soon found that there wasn't much to do since the Confederacy had no national court system, only state, county, and municipal courts.

However, Benjamin did get involved with the military preparedness for the conflict he was sure would come. He advocated the government purchase as much cotton as it could find, at least 100,000 bales, and ship it to Great Britain in exchange for 150,000 rifles and ammunition. Others in the Cabinet were against this idea since they thought the war wouldn't last long, so the arms were not purchased. This was a mistaken assumption that many Southerners made about the course the war would take. The belief was that there would be a few glory-filled battles, and then the United States would accept the legitimacy of the Confederacy.

While Benjamin was Attorney General, the Secretary of War was Leroy Walker, from Alabama. Many regarded him as disorganized, a poor administrator, and not well-suited for the job details. Walker had issued a call for 360,000 troops to be enlisted, but lacking arms to equip them, many were sent home. Had the arms been purchased as Benjamin had suggested, events at this early stage might have taken a different turn.

Benjamin had wanted to be Secretary of War when he was appointed Attorney General. But his loyalty to Davis required him to accept that appointment. After it became clear Walker was not up to the task, Benjamin stepped into the job. Walker resigned after the First Battle of Bull Run (Manassas) over criticism of not following up on the rebel victory by pursuing the retreating Union army.

Benjamin became Secretary of War for the Confederacy in November of 1861, a role he was not well suited for since he had never been in military service, a fact of which he was acutely aware. Benjamin viewed the job as being very much involved with foreign affairs. He realized that the South was not the industrial power that the Northern states were. The South didn't have the manufacturing capability to equip an army rapidly. He felt he needed to look towards Great Britain and France for assistance. He was thorough from an administrative standpoint, but soon he began clashing with his generals, especially Generals P. G. T. Beauregard and Thomas "Stonewall" Jackson, over things he had no experience with. Benjamin came under harsh criticism from the press and the rebel states over the war's lack of men and supplies. Some criticized him as being too assertive, and others as not being assertive enough.

Another event that Benjamin was criticized for was the decisions involving the defense of Roanoke Island, North Carolina, in February 1862. In this battle, 3,000 Confederates faced 10,000 Union soldiers. The War Department had failed to provide adequate reinforcements and munitions, nor did they offer to evacuate the island when it was apparent the defense was futile. As a result, the Confederates escaped with only a few hundred men. The rest were killed, wounded, or captured. This loss threatened the port of Norfolk, an important naval installation for the Confederacy.

One of his more controversial acts as Secretary of War happened in East Tennessee when a group of insurrectionists who were against the Confederacy began burning bridges and cutting off access to the surrounding area by sabotaging the railroad. President Davis ordered Benjamin to deal with these Unionists, and after some discussion with Davis, he issued the order. The insurrectionists not proved to be bridge burners were to be held as prisoners of war, while the others were to be tried summarily by drumhead court and, if found guilty, executed on the spot by hanging. He added, "It would be well to leave the bodies hanging in the vicinity of the burned bridges." This decision would haunt Benjamin for years.

All these problems as Secretary of War led him to resign from this post and to accept the open position of Secretary of State. His appointment came on March 17, 1862, and was quickly confirmed by the Confederate Senate. Judah Benjamin would hold this office until the end of the Confederacy and was the one he was best suited for. He had extensive legal experience, was a great orator, spoke fluent French, and traveled to France yearly to visit his wife. He would work hard to get military support from both France and Great Britain.

Benjamin had two main objectives as Secretary of State: to get recognition of the Confederate States of America internationally as a legitimate nation and to get support from France and England for the war effort. To achieve the first goal, success on the battlefield was needed. Winning battles would also convince England and France that the Confederacy could win the war. General Lee was able to win battles but not in a decisive way. This made Great Britain and France hesitate to recognize the Confederacy formally.

Southern cotton had kept textile industries in both Great Britain and France supplied with raw materials, and they were dependent on the South for cotton since no other suppliers could meet the demand.

Britain provided the Confederate military with arms and other war materials and sold arms to the Union army as well. However, since Britain had outlawed slavery some twenty years prior, there was no support from the textile industry for a slave-holding nation.

Napoleon III of France was reluctant to support the Confederacy and remained officially neutral throughout the war. Supporting the Confederacy would mean war with the United States. Also, France was unwilling to act without collaboration with Great Britain. The issue of slavery was not as crucial to the French government as it was to Great Britain, although the French populace was vehemently opposed to slavery. The idea of recognition by these two European powers ended forever with General Robert E. Lee's defeat in July 1863 at Gettysburg, the loss of Vicksburg, and control of the Mississippi River within days of each other.

In addition to his duties as Secretary of State, Benjamin also managed a network of spies. The network extended from Washington DC into the Northern states and Canada. He also had operatives in Great Britain. He was the head of the Confederate Secret Service.

The mission of these agents overseas was to plant fake news in the newspapers of Great Britain. These articles aimed to give false information about Confederate victories in the British and French papers, attempting to persuade them to recognize the Confederacy and hopefully become military allies. These efforts were in vain, as neither country was willing to declare war on the United States.

The agents also robbed Northern banks, plotted to burn hotels in Manhattan, and possibly to conduct some form of chemical warfare. Operatives tried to influence the 1864 Republican convention in Chicago to prevent the election of Abraham Lincoln and get a candidate elected who might be willing to accept the Confederacy and peace.

There were also implications of Judah Benjamin being involved in the plot to assassinate President Lincoln. Benjamin's agents in Montreal had met with John Wilkes Booth and given him money to fund a plot against President Lincoln that initially involved kidnapping him. These activities by Benjamin's agents would follow him for years after the war.

Chapter Three

The Fall of Richmond

The climactic offensive, the Siege of Petersburg[1], Virginia, was a series of battles over nine months, primarily trench warfare. The trench lines eventually covered thirty miles around Petersburg's east and southern outskirts. General Lee had finally met his match in General Ulysses Grant. Grant was relentless in his attacks and willing to accept the losses of men and materials, which Lee could not afford. General Grant had come to the attention of President Lincoln after his successes in the Western theater. He had made Ulysses Grant a Lieutenant General, a rank not occupied since George Washington. Grant was now the supreme commander of Union forces.

The initial clashes of infantry had begun in June of 1864 and continued for the next ten months. By then, Lee's army had been weakened by disease, desertion, and combat losses. Finally, as skillful as he had been in defense, Lee realized that he could no longer hold

---

1 The trench warfare tactics used at Petersburg would be a preview of things to come in World War One. With the improvements in artillery, the perfection of the machine gun, and the use of aircraft, Europe would be a killing ground for millions of soldiers in a few years.

back the Union forces and could not continue to sustain the losses in men and materials.

On March 3, 1864, Confederate troops intercepted a bold attempt by the Union to infiltrate Richmond and decapitate the Confederate government by killing the entire cabinet and Jefferson Davis as well. Union cavalry, led by Colonel Ulric Dahlgren, rode towards Richmond with orders to kill as many cabinet members as possible. The cavalry was also going to liberate Union prisoners of war near the capital. In the skirmish with rebel troops, Dahlgren was killed, and orders were discovered on his body.

This enraged Davis and Benjamin to the point where they ordered agents to conduct operations against Washington and to expand the South's conflict into Canada. All these efforts would be too little and too late since Richmond fell a year later.

The Confederate government attempted to negotiate a truce and settlement of the war on February 3, 1865. Three commissioners from the Confederate government, Vice President Alexander H. Stephens, Senator Robert M. T. Hunter, and Assistant Secretary of War John A. Campbell, met with President Abraham Lincoln and Secretary of State William Seward onboard the steamer *River Queen* at Hampton Roads, Virginia. Discussions centered around the issue of slavery and compensation for enslaved people if emancipated. Ultimately, nothing was decided, and Jefferson Davis announced that the Union would not compromise. The Confederate government would have to try something else to prevent their defeat and capture of the capital at Richmond.

One of the more controversial ideas proposed by the Confederacy was that of offering the enslaved people in and around Richmond emancipation in exchange for service in the defense of Petersburg.

The proposal would need to be ratified by the Confederate Congress very quickly if the troops were to be trained and equipped in time to supplement the dwindling regiments facing the Union Army in the trenches around Petersburg, Virginia. For the enslaved people, the offer was simple: freedom in exchange for military service in the Confederate Army.

On February 9, 1865, at the African Church in Richmond, a meeting was held to present the plan to the public. This church was the largest venue in the city, but it was still not large enough to hold the more than ten thousand people expected to attend. Some sat in the windows and relayed the message to people gathered outside. The Reverend Moses Drury Hodge opened the meeting with a prayer. The first speaker was Jefferson Davis, looking thin and weary as he walked to the front of the church. He spoke for an hour, and in his speech, he asked the people to sacrifice even more and to redouble their efforts to support the war. He left the pulpit to thunderous applause that went on for several minutes. Next was Judah Benjamin, who had been hastily revising his speech notes during Davis's speech. He knew this would be his most crucial speaking performance as Secretary of State.

He began by asking the people to sacrifice even more for the war effort by donating bales of cotton and tobacco to generate revenue for the war and food to the soldiers on the battle lines. He was building up his oratory for the final and most controversial request. Benjamin said, "I want one other thing. War is a game that cannot be played without men." He said bluntly that slaves should be emancipated, quickly trained, and equipped to fight. Reactions from the audience were mixed, some agreeing and others shouting, "No, never!" In the end, he had won the crowd over to the idea, but the result was that very few of the enslaved people took the Confederate government up on the offer. It made little sense for enslaved people to risk their lives in a bloody siege when the Union Army was approaching Richmond. All they needed to do was wait, and they would soon have freedom. Shortly after the meeting, this idea was widely ridiculed in the Northern newspapers and was seen as an act of desperation by the Confederacy. It was now only a matter of time before the thin gray line of war-weary Confederates in the trenches of Petersburg would break from the massive onslaught of the Union Army of General Grant.

Finally, Lee acknowledged to himself that defeat was inevitable, so he notified President Jefferson Davis in March of 1865 that he could not guarantee that the capital of Richmond would not be lost. Grant made a breakthrough of the Confederate lines on April 2, 1865, and entered the City of Petersburg on April 3. Richmond surrendered the same evening. General Lee now began a retreat with his tired, hungry, and ragged army of 20,000 men being pursued by a Federal army of 80,000 that would end at Appomattox Court House and the unconditional surrender of the Army of Northern Virginia on April 9. The total collapse of the Confederacy would happen rapidly in the coming days. It would cause President Davis and the government officials to relocate the capital further south by train immediately.

Chapter Four

The Confederate Government on the Move

President Davis was at St. Paul's Church in Richmond at Sunday service conducted by the popular Dr. Charles Minnigerode when he was handed a telegram from General Lee announcing "his speedy withdrawal from Petersburg" and that the city of Richmond should be abandoned. The President and Cabinet should flee the city to a safer location to the south. Davis left the church and went to his office, called a cabinet meeting, and instructed them to evacuate by nightfall. Present at the meeting were Judah Benjamin, Secretary of State; John Breckinridge, Secretary of War; George Trenholm; Secretary of the Treasury; John Reagan, Postmaster-General; and Stephen Mallory, Secretary of the Navy. Absent was Attorney General George Davis.

They all returned to their respective offices and resumed packing, removing records, and other effects. Word of the government's evacuation spread quickly in the city, and the streets were filled with men and their Black servants moving luggage and trunks of all sizes and descriptions out of the way of the advancing Union army.

The Confederate treasury amounting to $500,000 (nearly $9 million today) of gold bars, coins, silver bars, and copper coins were packed into boxes and loaded aboard the train under the supervision of Walter Philbrook, Senior Teller of the Treasury Department. This would be used to pay soldiers and any other debts incurred. Midshipmen from the Confederate States Naval Academy under their Commandant, Captain William H. Parker, would guard the valuable cargo. They had been rushed into service from their training ship, *Patrick Henry,* on the nearby James River.

The collapse of the Confederacy was complete, and Richmond was abandoned by the government by the evening of April 2, 865. General Lee had moved west and was fighting a rearguard action against a vastly superior force of Union troops under the command of his nemesis, General Ulysses Grant, but would surrender unconditionally in a week on April 9. Grant had proven to be more than a match for Lee, who had gone virtually undefeated until the battle at Gettysburg.

Richmond after the fire in April 1865

On the third of April, an order to burn all Confederate state military materials was issued by General Richard S. Ewell, including tobacco stored in warehouses. The purpose was to deny these supplies to the Union forces soon to enter the city. However, as Jefferson Davis later called it, the conflagration got out of control, and much of the city was destroyed.

President Jefferson Davis still had a hope of salvaging the situation, so initially, he saw his hasty departure from Richmond as merely relocating the government to a safer place until the Confederate armies, still in the field and unaccounted for, could be organized into a viable fighting force in the hope of a negotiated settlement of the war.

Richmond was now a city in the grip of panic. The town had been shelled relentlessly by the Federals, leaving smoldering fires, animal carcasses in the streets killed by artillery, and inhabitants loading up their possessions on wagons and evacuating. The number of people leaving Richmond was quite large, and traveling by railroad train since there were still tracks going south that the Union had not damaged. The scene at the station was one of chaos. Minor government officials trying to board the last two trains leaving the capital were rudely turned away.

The Confederate cabinet consisting of President Davis and his wife Varina, Judah Benjamin, John Regan, Stephen R. Mallory, John R Trenholm, and George Davis would be on the second train departing the city. The Vice President, Alexander H. Stephens, who had spent most of his term at his home in Georgia, was missing from the group. Secretary of War John Breckinridge stayed behind to help organize a rearguard defense to delay Federal troops and prevent them from catching up with the Presidential train.

Danville, North Carolina, April 3

The town of Danville, Virginia, is a few miles north of the state line with North Carolina. It was 140 miles from Richmond, with travel made difficult by the condition of the tracks and roadbed along the way, necessitating frequent stops for repairs. To add to the problems, there was the unknown location of the Union cavalry of General Phil Sheridan, who had been in the Shenandoah Valley, laying waste to anything of value in his path. Sheridan had rejoined Grant and was now pursuing Lee, heading towards Appomattox. The group took until late the next day to reach Danville.

After learning of the government's relocation to their city, the citizens held a town hall meeting to discuss a proper reception and accommodations for the president and cabinet. The belief at the time was that Danville could be the capital for the foreseeable future. Mayor J. M. Walker presided over the meeting, and adequate accommodation was arranged for the hundreds of refugees now in their city.

President Davis commented later that he received an "Old Virginia" welcome from the city officials. The offices of the Confederacy were given space in the Benedict House on Wilson Street, and the office for President Davis was located at Major W. T. Sutherlin's mansion on Union Street. There was turmoil and uncertainty about the future among the populace of Danville, which prompted President Davis to issue a proclamation: "I will never consent to abandon to the enemy, one foot of the soil of any of the States of the Confederacy. Let us meet the foe with fresh defiance and unconquerable hearts." It is doubtful that the proclamation had the desired effect of reassuring the citizenry. They may have been more concerned about the retribution that Union forces may hand out for harboring the rebel government.

The presidential party left Danville, headed to Greensboro, North Carolina, on April 10, and arrived the following day. At Danville, Davis learned that General Lee was formally about to surrender his army to General Grant at Appomattox.

Homeowner Wilmer McClean had moved his family from Manassas, Virginia, after the first major battle of the war there in 1861 to find a place away from the fighting. The war caught up with him again in 1865 when his home was used as the meeting place for General Grant and General Lee to sign the surrender documents.

Greensboro, North Carolina, April 11

The reception in Greensboro was much different than what the presidential party had experienced in Danville. The trains passed over a railroad bridge just minutes before it was burned by pursuing Federal soldiers. With the news of General Lee's surrender just a few days before and the presence in the state of Union General Sherman's "bummers," the local inhabitants were concerned about reprisals against the town and its citizenry if they provided aid and comfort to the "Rebel Chiefs" as the Federals called them. Therefore, none of the comforts and hospitality were offered to the party, and none of the homes were open to them except President Davis. The cabinet members had to make do with sleeping in an old railroad boxcar.

On April 13, a cabinet meeting was held, and the terms of Lee's surrender at Appomattox Courthouse were discussed. The details were brought by John Breckinridge, who had just caught up with the presidential trains after helping to organize the delaying tactics against their pursuers.

President Davis fared better with accommodations at Greensboro through the efforts of Col. John Taylor Wood. Wood was a naval officer and had been wounded in the pivotal battle of the ironclad war-ships *Monitor* and *Merrimack*. Wood's grandfather had been Zachary Taylor, an army general and twelfth President of the United States. Through marriage to his first wife, Davis was related to Wood, so he was intent on ensuring Davis got comfortable accommodations in the town.

Here, Davis learned the terms of General Lee's surrender at Appomattox via a letter from Lee himself. It drove him to the depths of despair. After consulting with cabinet members and his generals, they urged surrender unanimously. Davis refused to consider that option and pressed southward to get to Georgia and possibly head west to the Trans-Mississippi (Texas) region. The hope was that an army could be cobbled together from the remnants of units that had not yet surrendered and that the fight could continue.

With the imminent surrender of General Joseph Johnston's Army of Tennessee, Davis decided it was best for the government to continue to move further south. However, the Federal army controlled the railroad between Greensboro and Charlotte, so the only alternative was to travel by road on horseback and in wagons. Judah Benjamin, who was rather stout and not used to the physical exertion of riding a horse, protested vigorously. The presidential party left Greensboro on April 15 for a slow and arduous journey to Charlotte. Several traveled in ambulances (horse-drawn wagons); the rest, including Davis, were on horseback.

Charlotte, North Carolina, April 19

President Davis and his party arrived in Charlotte on April 19, 1865, and found the city crowded with many other refugees from Richmond. There, he was reunited with his wife, Varina, who had fled Richmond ahead of him. Benjamin had returned to his boyhood home but would not his spend time reminiscing. The response of the locals was reserved due to the presence of Union cavalry under General George Stoneman, who was wreaking havoc west of the Catawba River. Fears of retribution for harboring a much-wanted fugitive and his cabinet had the townspeople on edge. The fear proved unfounded as General Stoneman had turned west and away from the presidential party. Once again, good fortune had aided the fleeing Confederates and the treasury.

Davis called a cabinet meeting and discussed the pending terms of surrender for General Johnston to Union General Sherman. Davis had asked for written opinions on the terms of surrender, and all agreed that they were acceptable. However, the fortunes of the Confederate government would take a turn for the worse on receiving tragic news from Washington, DC.

President Abraham Lincoln Assassinated

President Davis received word at Charlotte by telegram of the assassination of President Lincoln, which had occurred on April 14. Lincoln, his wife, and guests had attended the play *"Our American Cousins"* at Ford's Theater in Washington that evening. The group of conspirators, led by actor John Wilkes Booth, had planned to assassinate President Lincoln, Vice President Andrew Johnson, and Secretary of State William Seward.

Lincoln was mortally wounded; Seward was seriously wounded in a knife attack, and Johnson escaped harm altogether. Most of the cabinet took this news as a blow to their cause. Davis later commented, "I certainly had no special regard for Mr. Lincoln, but there are many men whose end I would much rather have heard than this. I fear it will be disastrous to our people, and I regret it deeply." Lincoln had been more interested in reconciliation between the North and South than retribution.

Lincoln had commented that he hoped all the Confederate leaders would escape so that the reconciliation could begin without the many trials for treason that others would demand. Andrew Johnson, who was now President, was of the opposite opinion. He wanted to punish the South for starting the war. There was outrage by the Northerners over Lincoln's assassination, and the possibility of Davis and his cabinet's involvement was considered.

The Federal Army began a manhunt for the conspirators around Washington and arrested anyone who may have been involved in some way. Hundreds were rounded up and jailed until their innocence was proven. One person who was caught up in the dragnet was Dr. Samuel Mudd, who had treated Booth for a broken ankle sustained when he jumped from the balcony at Ford's Theater after shooting Lincoln. Dr. Mudd was later imprisoned at Fort Jefferson in the Dry Tortugas south of Florida for aiding Booth.

The conspirators' trials in the Lincoln assassination would reveal connections to Benjamin. His agents had given money to John Wilkes Booth in Montreal. Investigators had found a code cipher key among Booth's possessions that matched one found in Benjamin's abandoned Richmond office. Even more ominous was the employment by Benjamin of John Surratt Jr., the son of Mary Surratt, whose boarding house in Washington was used by the conspirators as a meeting place.

This turn of events made the escape even more hazardous for the presidential party. There was much concern for their safety when they were considered traitors to the country. Now, they had the added charge of possibly being involved in the assassination of the Great

Emancipator and the one person working to return the country to some state of normalcy. Ultimately, no link between Jefferson Davis and his cabinet to the assassination was conclusively proven. John Wilkes Booth and a small band of co-conspirators were responsible. But for now, this event added a sense of urgency to escape to the Trans-Mississippi region and safety.

Davis left Charlotte on May 26 after a dismal cabinet meeting where the subject of General Johnston's surrender of the Army of the Tennessee to General Sherman was discussed at length. Davis hoped to get to Georgia and then head west to Texas. This was no easy task since there were 13,500 Federal cavalrymen near Macon, Georgia, under General James H. Wilson, all searching for fleeing rebel leaders.

Abbeville, South Carolina, May 2nd

Abbeville was founded in 1764 by French Huguenots and named after a city in France. It was known as the birthplace of the Confederacy since the first convention for secession was held there, with South Carolina being the first state to leave the union. It was now going to be the deathbed of the Confederacy, with the last full meeting of the cabinet to decide the fates of the government and remaining armies taking place there.

After arriving at Abbeville, Davis had a private meeting with Judah Benjamin to discuss a plan for reestablishing the Confederate government in the west, preferably in Texas. Instead, Benjamin had a proposal of his own. That was for him to escape the United States through Florida and on to the Caribbean, reform the government with other Confederate refugees in Havana, and meet up with Davis in Texas later.

Benjamin had no intention of following through on his plan. He wanted to escape the United States permanently and was prepared, in his words, "to go to the middle of China" if need be. In a letter to his sister, Penina, he wrote, "Everything satisfied me of the savage cruelty with which the hostile government would treat any Confederate leader who might happen to fall into their hands, and I preferred death in attempting to escape, to such captivity which awaits me if I became their prisoner."

The last cabinet meeting at the home of Armistead Burt

The meeting was held in the home of Armistead Burt, an attorney and former US Representative. The house sat on a hill near the town square. This home had been built by David Lesley in the 1830s and was acquired by Burt in 1862. Until now, Davis believed he was moving the government away from danger and that the cause was not hopeless. He wanted to discuss the future with his cabinet and see what they believed was possible. This was a council of war from

Davis's perspective, and the attendees included all the military officers of his escort. The meeting was held between two and six in the
afternoon.

After a discussion, Davis made a radical proposal. He would use
the 3,000 men of his escort under General Breckinridge as a "nucleus
around which the whole people will rally when the present panic
has passed away." The idea was met with "dumbfounded …silence."
Colonel William Breckinridge (cousin of General Breckinridge) was
of the opinion "that there was no war to continue." Davis asked what
the 3,000 cavalrymen were for and got the response that they were to
ensure his safety and escape, if possible.

Breckinridge was adamant that they would not fight a guerrilla
war to continue the conflict. Once Davis had escaped, the cavalry
unit would disband and head for their homes with their mission
complete. This meeting indeed spelled the end of the Confederacy,
and Davis would be on his own. Davis's hopes had been dashed by
what he heard from the officers. He realized at this point that it was
truly over for the government and his term as president. He left the
room with shoulders slumped, lay down, and slept for a few hours.

According to Theodore Lesley, it was at Abbeville that Judah
Benjamin first contacted the Lesley family. He writes, "…the Secretary
had met members of the family, who directed him to their kinsmen
in Florida, including Thomas G. Livingston who met Benjamin in
Georgia, and would escort him into Florida and direct him to his uncle, Leroy G. Lesley". Leroy Lesley[1], now living near Ocala, Florida,
was born in Abbeville and had lived in Tampa before moving to

---

1 Leroy Gilliland Lesley was a minister, soldier, cattleman, and civic leader called
"the Fighting Parson," He is buried in Tampa's Woodlawn Cemetery.

Brooksville. He married Indianna Livingston, Thomas's sister, also from Abbeville. His son, John Lesley, still lived in Tampa.

Presidential party in Georgia. Benjamin is in the front.

The presidential party left Abbeville that evening, May, heading for Washington, Georgia. Most cavalry escorts departed for their homes after payment for their time of service, unwilling to go further. There had been open discussion among the cavalrymen about the chances of Davis and Benjamin escaping successfully. Most thought that Davis had the best odds and that Benjamin would most likely be caught. He was not in good physical shape and not used to living in primitive conditions or spending long hours in a saddle. When he departed the group at Abbeville, he was in a horse-drawn wagon.

Benjamin left the presidential convoy and headed to the south for Georgia. He had revealed to Davis that he had a false passport. It had been issued by an assistant to the Adjutant General, certifying him to be a French citizen, Jules P. Bonfals, which entitled him to travel "without hindrance from Southern forces." In addition to Thomas Livingston, he had Colonel Henry Leovy, a cavalry officer, as his traveling companion; he was a fellow Louisianan and lawyer who could speak French. This companion would play a part in the first of Benjamin's disguises that he would assume on his journey southward.

Benjamin and his companions soon descended the steep banks of the Savannah River and headed southwest. He may have considered this river crossing as his own personal Rubicon. He was going into uncertain territory without the protection of cavalrymen, surviving by his wits, a little luck, and the hope that he could find the right people who could help him on his way. There would be no turning back now, and he would need all the help he could get!

Washington, Georgia, May 3

Bank of the State of Georgia 1865

Benjamin, fearing that their capture by Federal cavalry was imminent, had left on May 3 before Davis's party reached Washington, Georgia. He was now moving south and west with Leovy and Livingston, who would guide them through Georgia on the back roads. Benjamin had been the source of entertainment, keeping everyone's spirits up. He had an endless supply of stories and anecdotes and delivered them with power and humor while puffing on one of his Havana cigars. He would not see Jefferson Davis again until many years later in London, although he would cross paths with several others in the party in the coming months. He intended to travel to Madison, Florida, and then look for a boat to leave the United States by traveling down the east coast of Florida.

The remainder of the presidential party entered Washington, Georgia, on May 3 with the treasury wagon under John Breckinridge's command. They crossed the Savannah River at Fort Charlotte Plantation, south of Vienna, on a pontoon bridge. Washington was home to several planters and had escaped the damages of war inflicted on other cities.

On May 4, Davis held a meeting in the bank building on the town square, courtesy of Dr. J. J. Robertson. Thus, the Bank of the State of Georgia became the site of the last official meeting of the Confederate government. At this meeting of Judge Reagan, Colonels, Wood, Lubbock, Johnston, Thorburn, and other staff members, Davis made his last appointment of Captain M. H. Clark as Acting Treasurer. Davis and his wife, Varina, would now continue south along with a small escort of twenty cavalrymen and a few remaining officials of the Confederacy.

Attorney Robert Toombs lived in the same town, his mansion barely a mile from the town square. He was a political rival of Jeff Davis and a staunch secessionist. He had been hoping to be chosen as the first president of the Confederacy, but Davis was chosen instead. The delegates tasked with selecting the new president in 1860 had been concerned about Toombs's drinking problem, his irascible personality, and his usually disheveled appearance. However, Davis did appoint Toombs to be his first Secretary of State. Toombs had been against starting the war and was the only person in Davis's cabinet to protest the attack on Fort Sumter. He believed that war was not inevitable but would be unwinnable and lead to the South's destruction. He refused to let Davis in his house as he was passing through, although he was willing to provide a horse or food to aid his journey.

Chapter Five

Jeff Davis's Capture

Judah Benjamin's concern that Jefferson Davis and his party would run out of luck came true not long after everyone separated in Washington a few days before. Davis had several things working against him at this point in the trip. The newly inaugurated President, Andrew Johnson, had placed a $100,000 ($1.8 million today) reward for his capture in the belief that Davis had been involved in President Lincoln's assassination. This greatly energized his pursuers, and there were plenty of them!

Davis was perhaps the most recognizable person in the Confederate government, so using a disguise was not possible. The others were less well known and could more easily pass through the countryside without being discovered.

The group had about twenty cavalry escorts but also two wagons. The wagons would slow them down and limit their travel route to established roads rather than smaller trails.

Thousands of cavalrymen were in the region, and Federal gunboats plied the waters of the Atlantic and especially the Gulf of Mexico. He was heading south towards the small town of Irwinville, which had changed hands from Secessionists to Unionists just a few months before.

The townspeople had passed a resolution declaring the county's return to the Union. Fed up with the war and the destruction everywhere in the South and wanting to get back to normal, the Unionists drove out the rebels, threatening to kill them if they returned. There was a genuine fear of Union retribution if they were found to be protecting Davis and his party. General William T. Sherman had "made Georgia howl "on his march to the sea, burning everything that could be of value to the rebels. So, the days of townspeople welcoming Davis with food, lodging, ceremonies, and speeches were over. He was now in hostile territory with a price on his head.

Traveling south towards Irwinville, the group crossed a small stream surrounded by a large marshy area. They were about a mile north of the town and decided to stop there, where they were away from inquisitive strangers and near a water supply. The party had covered thirty miles that day, and both men and horses were exhausted. They dismounted, set up two tents about one hundred yards south of the stream, and put guards around the camp. The group probably felt secure in this location and looked forward to spending the night under the tall pines and hickory trees surrounding them.

Cavalrymen from the 4th Michigan and 1st Wisconsin Regiments accomplished Jefferson Davis's capture. Each was on Davis's trail but unaware of the other's actions. Scouts from the 4th Michigan Regiment had ventured into Irwinville ahead of Davis's group and aroused the locals at 1:00 a.m., asking questions about the group north of town. Many townspeople were reluctant to talk, but one former slave was willing to tell all he knew. He said it was mounted soldiers with accompanying wagons, and nobody from the town knew who they were. The presence of wagons meant it wasn't another cavalry unit but some other group of people traveling with a military escort. The 1st Wisconsin cavalry was coming towards Davis's camp from the north on Abbeville Road, following the group, confident that it must be the presidential party.

Newspaper picture of Davis capture depicting him in women's clothes.

Each of the two cavalry groups was unaware of the location of the other and began firing at the other in the predawn darkness. Several were wounded, and three were killed in this "friendly fire" incident. The Michigan cavalry swarmed into camp as everyone was scrambling to their feet and coming out of their tents. Davis had grabbed what he thought was a blanket but was his wife's shawl. He ran towards the stream, hoping to get to the swamp and safety. When a cavalryman approached him and ordered him to stop, Davis considered pulling the man from his horse, mounting it, and riding away. The soldier leveled his pistol at Davis and prepared to fire. Varina Davis wrapped her arms around her husband, putting herself between the two men. Davis realized that it was finally over for him and surrendered. Newspaper articles and cartoons later depicted Davis wearing women's clothes to humiliate him for years afterward.

The rest of the Union soldiers began rounding everyone else up and began looting the wagons in search of the Confederate treasury rumored to be in the wagons. There was sporadic shooting from the cavalrymen until they figured out what was happening. Davis and the others were put on horses, escorted away, and headed on a four-day ride for Macon and the headquarters of General Wilson.

John Taylor Wood's Escape

Despite all the confusion, John Taylor Wood wandered around the campsite and pondered how to escape his situation. Wood was ordered away from his horse, and the animal led away. He then asked one of the Union cavalrymen, a German immigrant called "the Dutchman," to escort him to the edge of the camp so he could relieve himself. The soldier obliged, and when they were away from the camp, Wood turned and presented him with a $20 gold piece and said he didn't want to return to the camp. The soldier held up two fingers, indicating he wanted two gold coins in payment. Wood gave him the coins, turned his pockets inside out to prove he had no more money, and the soldier turned and walked alone back to the main group.

Walking quickly back into the swamp and finding a hiding spot, Wood lay down for about three hours to wait for the soldiers and others to leave. Wood could see Davis riding away under escort, his fate uncertain in the coming days and months. He could hear the soldiers talking amongst themselves, and they would bring their horses to the stream for water, which was close by.

John Taylor Wood

He heard the wagons leave first, and then bugles sounded for the cavalry to move away. After the site was deserted, Wood came out of the swamp and looked around for anything of use for his getaway. He saw someone leading two horses and recognized Captain Stephen Barnwell, one of the cavalry escorts. Barnwell was an artilleryman who had been wounded and had been in a hospital in Greensboro. His father, Senator Robert Barnwell, had been a close friend of Davis's, so he decided to join the group as they passed through Greensboro on their way south. Barnwell and Wood now worked together to continue their journey south.

Hiding the horses, which were tired and war-worn, the pair roamed the camp looking for bridles and saddles. They were able to gather enough to saddle and bridle the horses. A resident, Mr. Fenn, was given what was left of the food at the campsite.

Wood, along with Captain Barnwell, rode to Irwinville, a mile to the south. The townspeople mistook the pair for Yankees, and they were treated hospitably. They recommended going ten miles away to the home of a Widow Poulk, a cattle rancher of means, to spend the night. Wood had managed to save his haversack and its contents, along with a Derringer pistol he found at the campsite before leaving. He was now on his own and would continue to ride towards Florida, a few days' ride to the south. He planned to go to the east and try to find a boat on the Atlantic side of the state and escape to Cuba.

Chapter Six

Georgia

The Lesleys in Florida would be instrumental in Benjamin's escape, helping him more than anyone else except Frederick Tresca, a ship's captain and blockade runner, whom Benjamin would meet in the coming weeks. But that is for a later chapter!

The events of the last few weeks had turned his world upside down! Benjamin had been a successful attorney, plantation owner, businessman, and senator from Louisiana, and then held different posts in the Confederate government, the last office being Secretary of State. He had been a valuable assistant to Jefferson Davis and was called "the brains of the Confederacy."

Now, he wanted nobody to recognize him, and he had to create a credible new identity. Benjamin adopted the first of many disguises he would use during his escape. He had a suitcase with his initials "JPB," which stood for Judah Philip Benjamin. He came up with Jules P. Bonfals, a play on the Creole word "bonfals," which meant "good disguise." This way, it would match the suitcase's initials if anyone questioned him too closely.

Henry Leovy had been a cavalry officer at the war's end, serving with the Army of Northern Virginia under Lee. Leovy was acting as an interpreter to Benjamin, who was supposed to speak no English. In addition, Benjamin was wearing a floppy hat, goggles, and a heavy coat to make himself unrecognizable. He was riding in a rough carriage since he was not used to the rigors of riding long distances on horseback.

Benjamin, Leovy, and Livingston had been on their own for a few days, heading south through sparsely populated Georgia. They were unaware of the fate that had befallen Jefferson Davis and his escorts, but they would soon find out. Their group had passed Irwinville just a few days before Davis's party. Their travels were slowed by having to hide from the Federal cavalry, who were everywhere in the state looking for remaining Confederate fugitives. The rolling hills, deep ravines, and thick forests of pines, hickory, and oak trees provided plenty of cover to hide from the Federal patrols that roamed the countryside, and that could appear without warning.

After traveling for about two weeks, the trio of refugees heard the sound of horse hooves thundering upon them from the north. As the rider neared the group, they recognized him as John Taylor Wood. He rode up and announced excitedly, "Mr. Secretary, the President has been captured!" This was May 11, just a few days after Wood had been in Irwinville. Benjamin realized now that his situation was more desperate than he had thought. He needed to quicken his pace of travel to put as much distance between himself and his pursuers. Rumors of Federal troops in Madison caused Benjamin and his companions to change directions towards the west and enter Florida at Monticello. Hopefully, this would be far enough away from the Federal cavalry who were scouring the eastern part of the state.

Chapter Seven

Monticello Florida

T he devastation from the war, visited on other states in the Confederacy, mostly had been avoided in Florida. There had been only a few relatively small battles compared to states like Virginia, which had been fought there. The battles at Olustee and Natural Bridge were the largest, with less than five thousand combatants on each side. Tallahassee was the only Confederate capital not captured or damaged by the Union. Several forts along the coast had been occupied by the Union for the duration of the war, mainly to support the blockade and to disrupt the supply network of the south. Many salt distilleries had been destroyed, and some of the plantation sugar mills had been made inoperable, like the one at the Gamble Plantation. Several ships used by blockade runners had been sunk, burned, or seized by the Union for use as transportation.

The same couldn't be said for the Florida veterans of the Confederate Army and Navy. Casualties had been high among the fifteen thousand soldiers sent to the Army of Northern Virginia and Army of the Tennessee. Five thousand citizens from Florida joined the Union Army as well. So, even though Florida was firmly a secessionist state, there were many Unionists among its population.

As Judah Benjamin traveled through Florida and Georgia, he would encounter on the roads many Confederate veterans, some with injuries from the war, returning to their homes. On these same roads would be families of veterans who would stop anybody that they encountered, asking if they had any news about a husband, father, or son who had gone to war. In the towns, there were posters offering rewards for the capture of Jefferson Davis or Jacob Thompson[1] for their alleged involvement in President Lincoln's assassination.

Judah Benjamin had considered entering Florida at Madison. He planned to secure a boat and try to escape south along the east coast. But the rumor of Union cavalry in Madison and the lack of suitable boats in the area changed his mind. He went twenty miles to the west and entered Florida at the town of Monticello.

Established in 1827, Monticello was named after Thomas Jefferson's home in Virginia. The area was home to several plantations that helped keep the South supplied with food and cotton during the war. Monticello had largely avoided the destruction experienced by other towns in the South. Traveling down the Waukeenah Road, through rolling hills and farmland, the party, now without Thomas Livingston, would come to the Bellamy Road. The Bellamy Road, which would play a part in the route that Benjamin would now travel, was a mere ten miles south of the town of Waukeenah. This little village was known as a resting place for travelers on the Bellamy Road. The name is not native American in origin but Spanish. It is an Anglicized version of the name "Joaquina." John G. Gamble had built a planta-tion nearby named Joaquina. At this location the Bellamy Road went

---

1 Jacob Thompson was Inspector General for the Confederate Army and led a secret delegation to Canada. He conducted operations in the North from there. He is thought to be an associate of John Wilkes Booth

by the local name of the St. Augustine Road, of which there is a five-mile stretch remaining that runs parallel to U. S. Highway 27.

Author's photo of the Bellamy Road near Alachua, FL

The Burch-Bellamy Road was the first US Highway in Florida. Authorized by Congress in 1824, the road was named after Daniel Burch and John Jack Bellamy, who were awarded the contracts to build the road. It followed the Spanish "Camino Real" or Royal Road from St. Augustine to Pensacola and passed through Tallahassee.[2] Bellamy's portion of the road was completed in 1826. Native peoples

---

2 Tallahassee was made the territorial capital in 1824 and was chosen because it was midway between Pensacola and St Augustine. The state constitution was drafted in 1838 in St. Joseph (now Port St. Joe) and was almost chosen as the capital. Tallahassee is a native American word for "old town" or "old fields."

had used the path before the Spanish. During the Spanish Period, many missions were built along the road. Later, it was referred to as the Bellamy Road; parts of it are still called that today.

The road was simply a dirt track that had been widened to twelve feet by cutting down trees as needed. The stumps were cut below the height of wagon axles and were cupped to cause rainwater to pool and thus speed rotting of the stump. Marshy areas could be drained and banked, or logs could be placed to form a corduroy section of the road.

Henry Leovy[3], his traveling companion for several weeks, decided to separate from Benjamin at this time. One account stated that Leovy went to Tallahassee to sign his parole papers before continuing to his home in New Orleans. Confederate soldiers were required to sign documents stating that they would not bear arms against the United States again and were thus "paroled." This would permit them to travel freely back to their homes.

Tallahassee was twenty-five miles from Waukeenah, an easy day's ride on horseback. For Judah Benjamin, his hope for escape led to the east, towards the crossing at the Suwannee River. Judah was now without his assistant in his disguise as Mr. Bonfals, so he would need to come up with another ruse as he continued south. His inspiration for the new disguise would soon arrive at the Suwanee River.

---

3 Leovy would return to New Orleans and resume his practice of law. Later, he became vice-president of the New Orleans Bar Association and was vice-president of the Association of the Alumni of the University of Louisiana for many years."

Chapter Eight

The Suwanee River

Judah Benjamin continued east on the Bellamy Road and, according to most of the narratives, stopped at the home of Lewis Moseley for one night on May 14. Benjamin used a map drawn by Lieutenant Robert E. Lee when he was on the Board of Engineers (forerunner to the US Army Corps of Engineers) many years prior. The actual crossing of the Bellamy Road is at Charles Spring. I used the Bureau of Land Management's General Land Office records website to sort things out.

Charles Spring derives its name from the earliest white settlers in the area, Reuben and Rebecca Charles, who came to the banks of the Suwanee River in 1824. They had received information that the proposed Bellamy Road would be crossing in the area since this was a part of the old Spanish Royal Road. Reuben Charles had been familiar with the area since 1817 when it was a Spanish possession. He purchased eighty acres that included the spring in 1820, set up a trading post and ferry service, and could live peaceably with the local tribes since the family had traded with them for several years prior. Legend has it that the local tribe members would not harm them if they wore a red bandana to denote that they were friendly.

They lived in relative harmony with the locals, but Reuben was killed while walking along the Suwanee River around 1840. It was possibly mistakenly done by local tribesmen unfamiliar with the significance of the red bandana. Misfortune followed the Charles family when Rebecca was shot and killed while standing on her front porch. It was likely done by local whites who were hostile towards her for her friendliness with the local tribe members. The Charles family's descendants operated the ferry and trading post until 1870.

Louis M. Moseley, a former Confederate soldier, owned land adjacent to the property of Reuben Charles, but most of his land was on the east side of the Suwannee River. The US government granted him eighty acres in 1858 after serving in the Florida Militia during the Seminole conflict. This grant included a small parcel of land on the west side of the river, about one and a half miles south of the Bellamy Road, where it crosses the river. He operated a ferry service there. So, the narratives about Judah Benjamin spending one night with Moseley on May 14 and then crossing the river the following day are most likely authentic. Benjamin would have possibly revealed his identity to Moseley and asked for assistance on his journey.

Benjamin could have resumed his journey on the Bellamy Road since the road goes very near the river on the east side. It would be easy for him to find it. Just a few days after Benjamin had stayed there, John Taylor Wood and John Breckinridge spent the night with Moseley as well, so it appears that Moseley was well-known among the fleeing Confederates.

After crossing the dark tannic water of the Suwannee River, Benjamin would have entered lush forests of live oak, river birch, pine, hickory, and wild azaleas. Numerous springs dot the area; most likely, he would have availed himself of the cool waters, always 72 degrees. The terrain would become rolling hills for the next few hundred miles.

The Bureau of Land Managements' General Land Office records revealed another very interesting bit of information. The landowner directly to the south of Moseley's property was a man named Charles Howard. Judah Benjamin needed a new identity to replace Mr. Bonfals, which he had to give up because of Henry Leovy heading west towards Tallahassee less than a week prior. I think it's more than a coincidence that Benjamin chose "Charles Howard" as his new moniker. The timing is right, and the real Charles Howard and his wife probably assisted in his new disguise by providing rough homespun clothing and a mule so that Benjamin would look like a farmer from South Carolina seeking land in Florida to purchase.

Remnants of the Bellamy Road still exist in this area, giving clues to his possible travel route. Where the road passes through present-day Alachua County, it crosses over a natural land bridge across the Santa Fe River. The natural bridge is three miles wide and is located between the Oleno State Park and River Rise State Preserve. The road passes through the old county seat of Newnansville[1] and slowly turns southward, heading towards Gainesville. At some point between these two towns, Benjamin would have left the Bellamy Road and continued on whatever trails he could find on his way southward to Ocala.

The new Charles Howard traveled on his way east and south, with his next documented stop at the town of Ocala. There, he would

---

1 Newnansville was founded in 1814 and was named after the War of 1812 hero Daniel Newnan. It was made the county seat of the newly formed Columbia County. A land office was established there in 1842 to save landowners traveling to St. Augustine to file claims. It was bypassed by the Fernandina to Cedar Key railroad, and the town population declined. Nothing remains of the settlement today except two cemeteries.

find friends and get a little rest from the primitive conditions of his journey. He would catch up with Wood and Breckinridge there. He would have to leave the Bellamy Road since it continued east towards St. Augustine, and Benjamin wanted to avoid the east coast of Florida as an escape route. The roads going south were little more than trails, and Benjamin's actual route was uncertain at this time of his journey.

Chapter Nine

Ocala

The town of Ocala was named after the Ocali tribe of Native Americans living there. Initially, the county seat was Fort King, built in 1827. When the town was established in 1846, two miles west of the fort, the county seat was moved there. At the start of the Civil War in 1861, there were approximately 1200 inhabitants. By 1865, the town had been reduced to about 200, with the residents leaving the area for several reasons related to the war.

When Judah Benjamin arrived there in May of 1865, he met with one of many former Confederate Army officers who would assist him in his perilous journey to get out of the country. That officer was Brigadier General Robert Bullock, who had a home there. He also ran into John Taylor Wood and John C. Breckinridge, whom he had just missed by a few days at Moseley's Crossing. The local ladies there assisted all three fugitives by sewing in hidden pockets for them to carry gold coins to fund their journeys.

There was a small community of Jewish immigrants of Prussian origin, which formed around 1860 in Ocala. They started a synagogue and established a small cemetery; most were merchants.

Robert Bullock

He spent at least one night with a man named Solomon Benjamin, who has been incorrectly identified as his brother. In some written accounts, Solomon was called a "kinsman" or "relative," a term with several meanings. It can be a blood relative, a person related by marriage, or someone of the same nationality or ethnic origin. By examining Solomon's ancestry, I found that he was not Judah's brother but someone who had the same name as his brother. How Judah Benjamin knew of Solomon, or even the Jewish community, is unknown. He may have known Solomon personally or been introduced by General Bullock. Benjamin may have felt they would give him shelter and food on his way south.

Robert Bullock's home in Ocala

Solomon Benjamin had a brother named Simon, and they were merchants who were later involved with building a railroad line that went from Ocala to Silver Springs after the war. Solomon is listed on the 1870 census of Marion County.

Benjamin continued southward after his short stay in Ocala, his next destination being Brooksville, fifty miles southwest of Ocala. He would meet with the Lesley family and begin the next part of his journey with their help. John Taylor Wood and John Breckinridge still had a keg of gold coins, and they would head east past Silver Springs and down the St. Johns River to Lake Monroe and eventually make it to the Atlantic coast and out of the United States. The three would meet again in Cuba in the coming months.

Chapter Ten

The Parrot

Benjamin had been on the journey for some time now, traveling at night when possible and avoiding the busier roads. When he took time for sleep, he would move off the road so that he wouldn't be found easily. Since crossing the Suwannee River and departing the Bellamy Road, the route became little more than seldom-used trails passing through mosquito-infested marshlands. He was sometimes unsure if he was heading in the right direction. One morning, he was awakened by a high-pitched voice that said, "Hi for Jeff!" He shook off his sleepiness and looked around for the person calling out. Finally, he saw a parrot perched up in a nearby tree, which kept repeating, "Hi for Jeff." It seemed to Judah that this bird belonged to someone as a pet and certainly lived somewhere nearby. Benjamin also concluded that the owner must be a Confederate sympathizer since "Jeff" was most likely Jefferson Davis[1].

Benjamin was weary of traveling and sleeping in the bushes on the ground, so he saw an opportunity for better accommodations

---

1 This story appeared in several references about Judah Benjamin's journey through Florida. It is not known exactly where in the state it happened, but it was likely before he arrived in Brooksville.

if the owner could be found. Even though it was risky to search for someone in this wilderness area, he was tired of eating whatever food he could find and possibly encountering wild animals, which were abundant in the sparsely inhabited state.

He began throwing pebbles at the bird, not to hit it, but to cause it to fly away and hopefully return to its home and owner. The ploy worked, and Benjamin found the owner, who lived in a small cabin in the woods. He approached the man with caution and introduced himself as Charles Howard. His assumption of the man being a loyal Confederate was correct. He was able to spend a night in better circumstances and enjoy a little company before resuming his journey south. Soon, he would reach the town of Brooksville and meet up with friends who would play an essential part in his journey for the next few months.

Chapter Eleven

Leroy Lesley in Brooksville

Benjamin arrived in Brooksville with the letter of introduction that he got from Thomas Lesley at Abbeville, South Carolina, a few weeks before, requesting assistance in his travels. Benjamin had crossed the Suwanee River just four days before and was eager to continue. He inquired with the locals about how to find Leroy Lesley, and he was informed that Lesley's property was six miles south of the town. The plantation was known locally as the Ellis Place, and Lesley acquired it from Theophilus Higginbotham in 1863. Benjamin met with Captain Leroy Lesley, made his real identity known, and produced the letter he had gotten from Lesley's relatives. Lesley and Benjamin discussed options for routes through Florida. The best chance of escaping the country was through the village of Manatee and on to Cuba by sailing vessel. There was a lack of suitable boats on the Atlantic Coast and too many Navy ships patrolling those waters on the lookout for fleeing rebel leaders.

Benjamin expressed concern that the weak Spanish government in Cuba would not offer him protection, and he preferred one of the British islands in the Bahamas. Benjamin was now in the formation of a plan that would eventually get him out of the United States and onto British soil. He still had a long way to go, and there were plenty of dangers and uncertainties between Brooksville and Manatee.

Leroy G. Lesley

Leroy Gilliand Lesley had a long history in Florida. He was born in Abbeville, South Carolina, and moved to Madison County, Florida, in 1829. In 1834, he married Indianna Chiles Livingston, also born in Abbeville. Her parents, Thomas and Nancy Livingston, had died when she was a child, so she had lived with her brothers, Thomas, Madison, and William. Leroy moved to Tampa in 1848 after the "Great Gale of 1848", a Category 4 hurricane that had devastated the town. He had become a Methodist minister, and his church circuit included Hillsborough County. He fought as a captain in the Third Seminole War and commanded 124 men. He became known as the "Fighting Parson." The outbreak of the Civil War a few years later brought Lesley back to military service with a company of volunteers as a home guard. His son, Captain John T. Lesley, served as well, commanding 135 men in Company B, 1st Battalion Florida Special Cavalry, operating around present-day Plant City. John Lesley would be elected the twelfth mayor of Tampa after the war.

Lesley sent for his son John, who lived in Tampa, and it was decided without further delay to follow their outlined plan. Captain Lesley guided his companion southward through present-day Hernando and

John Lesley

Pasco Counties and eventually into Tampa. There, they would make contact with James McKay, who was a ship's captain and blockade runner. He had a home near John Lesley. The pair would continue the journey through Hillsborough County after landing on the bank of the Alafia River, east of Tampa Bay.

Morris Bridge crossing at the Hillsborough River. Photo by Author

Chapter Twelve

The Hillsborough River

After leaving Brooksville with John Lesley, Benjamin's next stop was near the site of the present-day town of Blanton, about twenty-seven miles north of Tampa. It is a small town in the rolling hills west of Dade City that would be formally established in 1884. The area had long been inhabited by a tribe of Seminoles who had migrated from Eufaula, Alabama. The area was called "Toadchudka" by the Seminoles, which translates to "muddy waters." The road going south from Brooksville was called the Toadchudka Road or Trail and was later known as Handcart Road, which parts of it are still called to this day. Other road sections are now called Happy Hill Road and Prospect Road.

Benjamin spent at least one night in the area, but whether he knew someone there is unknown. Present-day Blanton is about a day's travel from Tampa by horseback. Benjamin intentionally kept off the more heavily traveled roads, using Handcart Road instead of Fort King Road.

The road was little more than a dirt track through the countryside. The hills around Handcart Road slowly gave way to pine wooded flatlands. This part of Benjamin's route is Morris Bridge

Road[1], which starts south of State Road 54. When Benjamin passed there, it was called Jones Bridge Road after a settler named Ed Jones. He had acquired land near the Hillsborough River and called it Jones Hammock. He was a slave owner, and they built a dirt causeway and bridge so he could access his land. The exact location of the hammock is not known. As the road neared Tampa, it crossed Cowhouse Creek (or Slough) and continued south to Harney Road. It is unknown if there was a bridge here, but it's likely. This would have been the best route into Tampa at that time.

Cow House Creek

---

1 Jones Bridge Road was renamed Morrison Bridge Road and later changed to "Morris" Bridge Road. This is likely a mispronunciation that, over time, became the name most used.

A Hillsborough County map from 1882 shows Jones Bridge Road and the bridge's location at the Hillsborough River. Present-day Harney Road had no name then, but it is on the map. This dirt road makes its way into Tampa from the northeast. During this part of the trip, John Lesley met with James McKay and introduced him to Judah Benjamin.

Chapter Thirteen

James McKay in Tampa

James McKay, Sr.

James McKay Sr. was born in Scotland in 1808 and emigrated to Florida in 1837, as did many of the local inhabitants in Hillsborough County in the early 1800s. He opened a general store on Franklin Street in Tampa and a sawmill on the Hillsborough River. McKay also invested heavily in real estate in the area and eventually purchased two schooners that he used to transport goods to and from South and Central America, Cuba, and Florida.

In 1858, McKay began purchasing large herds of cattle for transport to Cuba and, in the process, became one of the area's wealthiest inhabitants. In 1859, he was elected as the sixth mayor of Tampa, but his term was cut short by the outbreak of the Civil War.

He was one of the original ship captains, along with Frederick Tresca and Archibald McNeil, to begin operating in the Gulf Coast region. When the Civil War broke out in 1861, the Federal Navy and Army began a blockade of the Southern states from Virginia to the Gulf Coast of Texas. It was dubbed "The Anaconda Plan" after the snake that strangles its victims. This action created much resentment among captains since beef, pork, salt, and sugar were necessary to feed the Confederate Army. They all became blockade runners, a very lucrative business that posed personal risks and maritime hazards.

Salt was a vital commodity in the South to preserve meat and tanning leather. Salt was so necessary during the war that hundreds of salt distilleries sprang up along the Gulf Coast to accommodate the increased demand. According to the New York Herald at the time, "Saltworks are as plentiful in Florida as blackbirds in a rice field." These distilleries would boil seawater in large vats to get the salt. Any person who could produce twenty bushels of salt daily would be exempted from military service in the Confederate Army. The distilleries were primarily operated by slave labor as it was hot and backbreaking work, and hordes of mosquitos plagued the workers. These distilleries were frequent targets for the Union blockaders, and because the sites needed to be near the coastline and required fires for boiling, they were easy to find. After being destroyed by the Navy, the distilleries would quickly be rebuilt.

In 1863, Confederate Major Pleasant W. White appointed McKay to the post of Commissary Agent for the 5th District of Florida. Archibald McNeill was his deputy in the Manatee area, and he lived in the Gamble Plantation house and operated the sugar mill there.

Some blockade runners, like Tresca and McNeill, avoided capture during their many trips through the blockade. James McKay was not so fortunate. McKay was captured, and his ship, the *Fargo*, was seized by the Federal Navy on June 7, 1861, while on the way to Cuba. He was released but captured again on October 14, 1861, with arms and munitions on their way to equip the Confederacy. McKay was imprisoned at Fort Jefferson in the Dry Tortugas and freed after taking the oath of allegiance to the Union as a condition of release after five months of captivity.

McKay met Benjamin when he was brought to Tampa by John Lesley. Lesley's home was a few miles outside of town, and most likely, Benjamin spent a few nights there in relative safety. Eventually, by one account, Benjamin went to McKay's home even though it was very near Fort Brooke. Fort Brooke had been a Confederate stronghold for much of the war, and they successfully defended it twice against Union attacks. However, on May 6, 1864, Union forces occupied the fort and would remain there until 1869.

McKay wanted no part in trying to get Benjamin out of the country and suggested he go to the Gamble Plantation and seek a way out of the country there. It had to be very dangerous to have the fugitive Confederate Secretary of State in a town filled with soldiers. Certainly, Benjamin would only move about after dark so as not to be easily recognized.

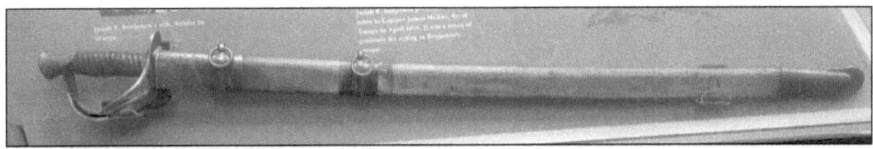

Sword given to James McKay. Author's photo

McKay transported Benjamin during a heavy storm across Tampa Bay, heading south towards Parrish. He would have anchored in the Alafia River and put Benjamin and John Lesley ashore to continue their journey. Before departing Tampa, Benjamin gave McKay a sword to show his appreciation for his efforts. The sword was donated to the Florida Park Service and is now displayed at the Gamble Mansion Historic Site Museum.

After the war, McKay resumed his cattle operations until he died in 1876. His son, James McKay Jr., served as mayor, and another son, John A. McKay, served on the city council.

Chapter Fourteen

Parrish

William Iredell Turner

J udah Benjamin was now at the bank of the Alafia River, where he met with William Iredell Turner[1], who had received advanced notice of his arrival. Captain Lesley and Benjamin rode to the home of Major Turner, a former Confederate militia officer from Hillsborough County. The plantation was twenty miles south, along the Tampa to Manatee Road,

---

1 William Turner was a soldier during the Second Seminole War and the Civil War. He was commander of Ft Brooke in Tampa for a short time during that war and later commanded Turner's Independent cavalry C.S.A., where he served as a major. He is credited with naming Gainesville. He led Palmetto's founder to that location, established "Braidentown" and was the town's first postmaster. He was chairman of the first Manatee County School Board. He was a Manatee County Commissioner and formerly a state senator from Hillsborough County.

a day's travel from the Alafia River. Turner was the owner of the Oak Hill Plantation. The plantation was in the center of present-day Parrish[2]. Turner offered to let Benjamin stay at his home till arrangements could be made and the route to the Gamble Plantation a short distance away secured.

The land had originally been acquired by William Hooker, along with William H. Johnson, in 1850, from the US government, and the plantation was established. They grew sea island cotton as the main crop. This variety of short-staple cotton, grown in coastal areas, became the prime commodity crop of the developing Deep South, and "King Cotton" was the basis of southern wealth in the antebellum years. The area featured relatively flat land with areas of marshy hammocks. There were live oaks, cabbage palms, and palmettos. The Manatee River was just four miles to the south and was a major transportation route.

In 1865, William Turner became its occupant and named it "Oak Hill." Benjamin was brought to the site by Captain Lesley, and he hid in a nearby swamp for a couple of days. One account related that a federal patrol that was on Benjamin's trail came to the Turner house and searched it thoroughly for hours but found nothing to indicate Benjamin's presence.

Visiting the Parrish Cemetery, I stood on a small hill next to a marshy area to the south. I wondered where the Turner house might have been but I have found no documents revealing the site. Alice Turner Berry inherited the cemetery property from her father, William I. Turner. Upon her death, it became the Parrish Cemetery. Was I standing at the location of Turner's House? Was the marshy

---

2 The town of Parrish was named after Crawford Parrish, who purchased the property from William Iredell Turner in 1870 and established a settlement.

area to the south the fugitive Confederate Secretary of State's hiding spot? It will probably never be known for sure. There is a large historical marker at the cemetery that details the story.

Captain Lesley, meanwhile, went alone to the Gamble Plantation and made arrangements with Archibald McNeill for a "Mr. Howard" to stay there. Benjamin's true identity would not be revealed till his arrival at the Gamble Plantation, only eight miles away on the bank of the Manatee River near present-day Ellenton. Even though it was a short distance away, the area had been searched by Federal troops that were trying to catch any of the Confederate leadership escaping through the state. Judah Benjamin's luck in evading capture would soon be tested at his next stop.

The Gamble Plantation

Chapter Fifteen

The Gamble Plantation

The Gamble Plantation was built by Robert Gamble Jr. between 1845 and 1850, primarily with slave labor. He had moved to Florida from Virginia and modeled his home after the plantations there. It is designed in the Doric Revivalist Vernacular style. However, he didn't have easy access to the same construction materials, such as marble and red clay bricks, so the Florida home was built with bricks made with tabby, a locally sourced material.

It had eighteen two-story columns and porches around the front of the house on both floors. The walls were three feet thick, so even though the building appeared large, the rooms inside were relatively small. Tabby insulates very well, so the house is comfortable in the hot summers of Florida. Large windows on opposing sides of the house allowed for good cross ventilation, and tall ceilings kept the rooms at a comfortable temperature. The kitchen and slave quarters were built first at the back of the house; the remainder of the house was built later. A large cistern on the east side provided clean drinking water for the family and enslaved people.

The property overlooked the Manatee River, about a quarter of a mile south. It would have been the main transportation route for his products, as waterways were the primary method throughout the state for moving cargo. Gamble had felled the trees around the house and down to the riverbank to prevent wildfire from endangering the house and other buildings. It also allowed the mansion's residents to observe the river for federal patrols during the war. Gamble operated the sugar mill till 1856. At its peak, it was 3,500 acres and employed 200 enslaved people. He had to sell the property due to crop losses caused by storms, competition from Cuban sugar producers, and the accumulation of debt.

During the Civil War, Archibald McNeill was the occupant, and the plantation was again producing molasses from sugar cane, now for the Confederacy. McNeill was a ship's captain and had been successful as a blockade runner. He was Assistant Commissary Agent in the Manatee District under James McKay in Tampa. The property was owned by John Cofield and Robert Davis of New Orleans, but they had ceased mortgage payments, and the mill was now "owned" by the Confederacy.

The plantation had been raided once by federal troops, with the sugar cane being cut down and the house ransacked in search of McNeil. In 1864, Commander Theodore Green of the East Gulf Blockading Squadron got word of this operation and mistakenly believed that the plantation belonged to President Jefferson Davis. Robert Davis was not related to Jefferson Davis.

Union sailors discovered the location of the sugar mill and machinery about a half mile north of the plantation house. The sailors placed artillery shells around the machinery and set the building on fire. The resulting explosion could be heard for miles. That ended sugar production at the plantation for good. The ruins of the mill buildings are still visible from the roadway today, although they are not open to the public and are now surrounded by a chain-link fence put up by the Florida Park Service.

McNeill had a bounty offered for his capture because of his activities for the Confederacy and was eager not to be found at the isolated location where he lived with his family. This was the situation at the Gamble plantation in the summer of 1865 when John Lesley rode from Parrish to arrange for a "Mr. Howard" to stay as a guest.

Benjamin and Lesley must have felt apprehension as they headed westward toward the Gamble plantation. Federal forces had been on Egmont Key since 1861, using it as a coaling station and hospital for East Gulf Blockading Squadron ships. The lighthouse had been used as an observation point looking for blockade runners. With the Gulf of Mexico, Tampa Bay, and the many rivers and waterways, federal forces would have easy access to the homes near the Manatee River that could be potential hiding places for the many Confederate fugitives thought to be heading south through Florida.

Lesley and Benjamin arrived at the Gamble plantation, and introductions were made. Archibald McNeill lived there with his wife Ellen and three small children, Charles, Fanny, and Sally. Another occupant of the mansion was Flora Vanderipe, her new baby, and her eight-year-old niece, Alice. Benjamin settled into a room on the second floor with a balcony overlooking the approach from the nearby Manatee River. Any Federals patrolling the river would come up the short road to the house, which was relatively isolated. Benjamin spent his days sitting in a rocking chair and keeping watch on the river.

Benjamin tried to convince McNeill to be the one to take him out of the country since he had been a blockade runner and sea captain in the area for many years. McNeil was reluctant to do so for several reasons. He had survived the war and didn't want to risk possibly being killed with Benjamin. He was afraid of being captured since there was a reward out for him, and he didn't want to be found with the former Secretary of State of the Confederacy, harboring a fugitive who also had a price on his head of $50,000 ($1.6 million today). McNeill was also a wanted man for his role in operating the sugar mill, which had supplied the Confederacy for years. McNeill needed to find someone else to take on this risky proposition of getting Benjamin out of Florida.

Judah Benjamin's bedroom. The doors in the back lead to the balcony, where he watched the river. Photo by author.

These were the conditions at the Gamble property, where he stayed for a few weeks. During the daytime, Benjamin would sit in a chair on the balcony next to his bedroom and look for Union gunboats with a spyglass. Things took a turn for the worse when, one day, Benjamin was not at his observation post on the balcony. Federal troops landed on the bank of the river and quickly headed up the dirt road to the plantation. By the time anyone at the plantation realized it, the troops were standing on the property's front lawn.

In a panic, Benjamin and McNeill ran out the back door, followed closely by McNeill's dog, and headed for nearby woods. Meanwhile, the women of the house rushed to the front yard and engaged the soldiers in conversation to stall them long enough for Benjamin and McNeill to find a hiding spot. The soldiers were suspicious of the sudden civility of these ladies when they were usually treated with hostility and distrust by the local inhabitants.

They began searching the house and then the surrounding woods. McNeill was afraid the dog would give their hiding place away, so he held his mouth closed and was ready to strangle him if need be. The soldiers came so close that the duo could plainly hear them talking; they were only a few feet away from them at one point. After several hours of terror on the part of McNeill and Benjamin, the soldiers reluctantly gave up the search and left at sundown. The fugitives came out of hiding in the woods and returned to the house. After this close call, McNeil took the added precaution of moving Benjamin from his bedroom into a storeroom in the back of the main house and above the kitchen. Benjamin later commented to a friend that the experience of nearly being captured was "exhilarating." McNeill was so rattled by this near disaster that he renewed his search for a captain for his guest. He said, "I have to find the Frenchman!" That Frenchman was a locally known and experienced ship captain, Frederick Tresca.

Preparations were made for transporting Benjamin across the Manatee River and eventually to Tresca's house, located one and a half miles south of the village of Manatee. The river crossing would be more than a mile and a half wide, so moving in the daytime was out of the question. Federal gunboats could potentially spot them from a great distance. Benjamin also needed new clothes, so Ellen McNeill sewed a blue denim suit and a pair of shoes out of an overcoat.

The exact circumstances of Judah Benjamin meeting Frederick Tresca have never been written about in any of the accounts I have found. Most likely, Benjamin would have moved to Tresca's property a short distance away. It is not as likely that Tresca and Benjamin would meet at the Gamble plantation as it would be a risky thing to do. Tresca and Benjamin possibly met at John Curry's home, and the pair went to Tresca's together. Curry would still have an important part to play in the next phase of Benjamin's escape.

Chapter Sixteen

Captain John Curry

John Curry

Captain John Curry (not to be confused with his son John William Curry) was one of the earliest inhabitants of the village of Manatee, going back to 1859 when he purchased thirty acres near the Manatee Mineral Springs[1]. He built two homes on the southern end of the property. His roots go back to Key West, where he began working as a ship's captain. He was also

---

1 Manatee Mineral Springs had been used for centuries by indigenous people and local settlers traveling in the area. In 2018, the site was recognized as a site on the Underground Railroad Network to Freedom for runaway slaves. In 2022, the park was re-landscaped, and a hand pump was installed in the spring.

a cattleman. John Curry was familiar with all the inlets and bayous where a blockade runner could hide. He also provided a schooner, *Ariel*, to the Confederate navy as a blockade runner.

Curry also had experience with the Union Army and their destruction of property that aided the Confederacy. They were responsible for sabotaging a grist mill and sawmill in the village Manatee[2]. They had been hidden in nearby woods but were discovered shortly before the sugar mill was found and destroyed at the Gamble plantation.

The entire area was a center for maritime activities. Nearby Fogartyville, Braidentown (Bradenton), and the village of Manatee had several captains who operated on the Manatee River and at shipbuilding and repair facilities. Captains like James McKay of Tampa, Frederick Tresca, and Archibald McNeill were acquaintances, all engaged in blockade running for the Confederacy.

After McNeill and Benjamin had nearly been captured at the Gamble plantation, plans were finalized to move him across the Manatee River and to Frederick Tresca's home to the south. Under the cover of darkness and with great secrecy, Judah Benjamin was taken to John Curry's home near the bank of the river. Curry rowed across the Manatee River to the north shore and picked up Judah Benjamin. He then rowed back across to his property near Manatee Spring.

It's not known if he arranged the meeting with Frederick Tresca. However, Tresca's home was about two miles from the Manatee Spring. Two of the homes built by Curry are still at their original location and have been preserved by Reflections of Manatee.

---

2 The grist mill and sawmill destroyed by the Union were jointly owned by John Curry, Josiah Gates, and Ezekial Glazier, founders and longtime residents of the village of Manatee, and mentioned in the next chapter. Troops from the 2nd Colored Regiment set up headquarters in one of John Curry's homes and an encampment nearby.

Captain Curry had hidden a sixteen-foot yawl[3] in the woods near the Manatee River to keep it from being seized or burned by the Union Navy. Some accounts say that the boat had been sunk in the river to avoid detection. This is unlikely since the boat would soon deteriorate to the point it would be unusable. This is the boat that Tresca would use to take Judah Benjamin to Knight's Key.

There is an alternate version of how Tresca acquired the boat he would use to travel from Whitaker Bayou. Several sources say that Tresca and Hiram McCleod had traveled overland to Clear Water Harbor (present-day Clearwater) and purchased the yawl. They then sailed from there to Whitaker Bayou to the south.

Although possible, I believe it to be unlikely since the trip would have been fifty miles long and traveling in an area home to a Union Navy coaling station on Egmont Key, which had many warships patrolling the coastline. The risk of capture by Federal forces would have been significant compared to the trip from the village of Manatee, which was only twenty miles, mostly in waters sheltered by barrier islands along much of the route.

An account of Tresca preparing to take a boat to Whitaker Bayou, written by the daughter of William Whitaker, has offered an explanation of Tresca's trip to Tampa Bay. She said that Tresca had "certain arrangements" that had to be made with the blockading fleet in Tampa Bay. He traveled to the fleet to obtain a fishing permit from the Navy.

Perhaps the Navy required a permit for captains to operate in an area under the control of the blockading fleet. While on this trip, he was asked and paid to transport two sailors from one of the ships,

---

3 A yawl is a single-masted, open sailboat, typically with one mainsail and a headsail in front of the mast.

whose enlistments had expired, to Tampa. Tresca felt he couldn't refuse the request.

On his return, Tresca hired Hiram McLeod as an assistant for the upcoming voyage since they had previously worked together. This caused a delay in the planning and eventual departure of Benjamin. This story, which has adequate corroboration, might be the origin of the s story of Tresca going to Clearwater to purchase a boat.

Chapter Seventeen

Frederick Tresca

Captain Frederick Tresca

Frederick Tresca and his wife, Louise Wyatt Tresca, lived on one hundred and forty acres south of the village of Manatee. Judah Benjamin would stay at this location in relative safety until further plans could be made for his next move.

Frederick Tresca had emigrated from his birthplace in Dunkirk, France, to the United States in 1838 and embarked on a career as a ship's captain, sailing between Key West along the Gulf Coast to New Orleans and south to Cuba.

He was also the lighthouse keeper on Egmont Key from 1856 to 1859, and he operated a rancho (trading post) in the Sarasota area, trading with the local settlers and the Seminole tribe.

Hiram McLeod

He was friends with Billy Bowlegs and was sympathetic to the plight of the Seminoles as they were being forced out of the state, some being interned on Egmont Key when he was the keeper there. During his time as keeper, his assistant keeper was Hiram McLeod, who would also play a part in Judah Benjamin's escape from Florida.

Tresca was the most qualified person to undertake the risky proposition of taking the Confederate Secretary of State out of the country. Tresca had been a captain, sailing in the Gulf of Mexico for many years, and was familiar with its many inlets, tributaries, and mangrove islands, which would be potential hiding places from Federal Navy patrols. He had lived in Key West for many years after arriving in the United States.

Also, Tresca had been a successful blockade runner during the Civil War, having made at least six trips to Cuba, just ninety miles off the Dry Tortugas in the Florida Keys. Benjamin offered him $1,500 (about $26,000 today) plus expenses to get him safely out of the United States and to British soil in the Caribbean. Having been born on St. Croix when it was in British possession, Benjamin could legally claim citizenship and would likely be safe from extradition.

Tresca's home was located near the present-day community of Samoset, south of the small village of Manatee, and was relatively safe

Ezekial Glazier

from Federal patrols. Judah Benjamin would be secure there, and the final planning and implementation of the escape from the U. S. could begin. Tresca enlisted the help of his friend and former assistant lighthouse keeper Hiram McLeod, whom he had known for many years.

Hiram McLeod had been a Confederate soldier during the war, mustering in at Shaw's Point, Florida. He had joined Captain John Lesley's Fourth Florida Regiment, Company K. During his service in the Western Theater of the war, he had been wounded in the right arm, suffered a shattered ankle, had a bullet lodged behind his kidney, and lost part of his left leg. But he was loyal to his friend Tresca and was eager to help with this new and risky endeavor of getting Benjamin out of the country.

To make the hazardous eight-mile journey from the Tresca home to William Whitaker's property near Sarasota, the assistance of Ezekiel Glazier and Jeffery Bolding, who had a connection to William Whitaker, was enlisted. When Florida became a state, Reverend Ezekiel Glazer settled in the Manatee area in 1845. He was a carpenter as well as a minister, and he had supervised the construction of Braden Castle and the first Manatee County Courthouse. During the Civil War, he had helped local families of Confederate soldiers. He was a delegate of the Florida Secession Convention in 1861 and had voted "aye" in favor of secession.

Jeffrey Bolding

Jefferey Bolding[1] was a former slave of Whitaker's who had stayed with him and continued to work for him after the war. Whittaker and his wife Mary Jane had found Bolding as a runaway from his owner in North Carolina, hiding in the scrub near Sarasota and near death after being there for some time. Whittaker and his wife nursed Bolding back to health and then located his rightful owner, intending to purchase him. He negotiated a price of $1000 ($35,000 today), and Bolding began a new life with the Whittaker family. He would remain friends with them for the rest of his life.

These two men were entrusted with the life and safety of the former Confederate Secretary of State and tasked with getting him safely to his next destination, William Whittaker's home at Yellow Bluff. To do this, extra precautions would be taken. The group was traveling in a two-wheeled open cart, so Benjamin must be hidden somehow. They decided to cover him with palmetto leaves and freshly butchered beef. The hope was that if stopped by a Federal patrol, they

---

1 Jeffrey Bolding married an enslaved person named Hannah, purchased by Whitaker. His loyalty to the Whitaker family was demonstrated when he carried Whitaker's son Furman home after he accidentally shot himself on a hunting trip. Jeffrey died in 1904.

would not be searched too closely, assuming nobody would be hiding under a pile of meat.

It's hard to imagine what it must have been like to travel any distance under such circumstances. He would be under a pile of smelly meat in near-total darkness and with difficulty hearing much of what may be happening. In addition to these preparations, additional riders went ahead of the cart and behind to intercept any federal patrols that may appear without warning. Fortunately for everyone involved, the elaborate ruse was not put to the test since no Federal patrols were encountered.

William Whitaker

Chapter Eighteen

William Whitaker

William Whitaker was born in Savannah, Georgia, in 1821 and had moved to his home near Sarasota by 1852, making him the first permanent white settler in the area. The land, 144 acres, had been acquired by Whitaker from the government under the Armed Occupation Act[1]. He later purchased another forty-eight acres.

His first home was a simple log cabin built near the Gulf of Mexico. He made his living by fishing and farming. He traded fish with the Cuban fishermen who had established fishing camps nearby. He became active in civic affairs as a clerk of elections. He was the first farmer to grow citrus in the county with plants he got from the Cubans.

The Whitakers were sympathetic to the plight of the local Seminoles and were friends with Billy Bowlegs. When the Third Seminole War broke out, that relationship ended, and soon, his cabin

---

1 The Armed Occupation Act of 1842 was an attempt by the government to encourage settlers to come to Florida and force the Seminoles out. The applicant had to be a white male, clear at least five acres of land and cultivate it, build a house on it, and be prepared to defend the land with force of arms, if needed, for five years. There were other conditions, and the person would be granted 160 acres when met.

was burned to the ground by the local tribe[2]. He was also sympathetic to escaped slaves, although he enslaved people himself.

When the Civil War started, the family was largely neutral about secession. He operated a grist mill with other locals hidden in the nearby woods. This allowed families to survive after Federal troops burned the steam-powered one near the village of Manatee.

The homestead, now rebuilt on what Whitaker called "Yellow Bluffs," was visited more than once by Federal troops. They would come ashore from Sarasota Bay, looking for livestock or other food-stuffs. Usually, they would offer to buy them, but if the farmer re-fused, they would take what they wanted.

Whitaker Home - Photo courtesy of the Manatee County Library

2 U. S. historians divide the Seminole Wars into three distinct outbreaks of military action spanning forty years. The Seminole Tribe of Florida is adamant that it was one long conflict with outbreaks of military action that lasted from 1817 to 1858, with periods of tense peace in between.

Once, the Federal troops threatened to burn the house, but Mary Whitaker was unafraid. A soldier took a rifle from Furman Whitaker, his twelve-year-old son, and Mary told him to go to the soldier's camp, find the officer in charge, and demand the return of the rifle, which was needed for hunting food. Young Furman did as his mother said, and the commanding officer returned the rifle with apologies.

Ezekiel Glazier, Jeffery Bolding, and Judah Benjamin had completed the treacherous nine-mile journey to the Whittaker property without encountering any Federal patrols. However, they were not out of danger in their new hideout. The proximity to Sarasota Bay and the Union Navy's easy access made this place's safety tenuous at best. The final planning needed to be completed quickly, the boat provisioned, and the journey continued on the waters of the Gulf of Mexico as soon as practical. The next step was to meet up with Frederick Tresca, Hiram McLeod, and the yawl they would use to make their escape.

The yawl (sometimes erroneously identified as the *Blonde*) acquired from John Curry in Manatee was sailed to Whitaker Bayou by Tresca and Hiram McCleod and hidden there. The bayou is a typical narrow, winding waterway with many overhanging trees that would have offered plenty of hiding places along its course for a small boat. The slow-moving water was tea-colored due to tannic acid from decaying tree leaves that fell into the water.

It's impossible to know exactly where the boat was hidden in the bayou, but it was less than a mile from the bayou to the Whitaker house. They waited at Yellow Bluff for Benjamin and his escorts to arrive from Tresca's house. The plan was to get provisions for the boat and for Tresca, McLeod, and Benjamin to set sail from Whitaker Bayou into Sarasota Bay and head south towards the Florida Keys.

Furman Chairs Whitaker, William's eldest son, recalled as a young boy seeing his father, Tresca, and Benjamin sitting on the tongue of a wagon in the yard of the Whitaker home. Furman remembers seeing the three men huddled together in a serious conversation under an old live oak tree. When relating the story, Furman understood they were planning something but couldn't recall details many years later.

Whittaker's wife, Mary Jane, prepared a large meal for the three men just before their departure. It was a nice gesture since it might be quite some time before they could have a satisfying meal in a peaceful setting like this.

Now, the three men would embark on what was to be the most hazardous part of the journey. They would be in a small sailboat in open water and unable to hide from the large numbers of Federal patrol boats steaming in the Gulf of Mexico, from Tampa Bay to the Union Navy coaling station in the Dry Tortugas. Food and fresh water would be scarce, the sun would be bright and hot, and the weather would be unpredictable. Judah Benjamin would soon need a new disguise for this part of his journey.

Joe and Julia "Madam Joe" Azeroth

The story of Joe and Julia, "Madam Joe" Azeroth of Palmetto, illustrates the determination of Union forces to track down Judah Benjamin. They were early settlers in the area and operated a farm and store for locals. They had owned a sloop called the *Mary Nevis,* which had been confiscated by the Union Army and pressed into service. They made several stops at the Azeroth property, looking for anything of value. The Azeroth's had hidden their food stores so they couldn't be taken as contraband.

Julia Azeroth

One day, the Union soldiers came to their store searching for Benjamin, who had already left the area. The soldiers were convinced that Madam Joe was Benjamin in disguise. She was rather tall and stout, had sun-weathered skin, and somewhat resembled the fugitive, given there was no photograph for comparison. The soldiers required her to prove she was a woman, but the details of how that was accomplished will be left to the reader's imagination!

Chapter Nineteen

On to Knight's Key

The trio of mariners set sail out of their hiding place in Whitaker Bayou on June 23, turning south through Big Pass in Sarasota Bay and heading into new uncertainties and challenges. The plan was to make landfall in the Florida Keys, more than two hundred miles away; the trip was expected to take two weeks. The Keys were sparsely populated in 1865 and would be a good launching spot in an attempt to get to the Bahamas.

The feeling of freedom from being on land and worrying about traveling on roads with the possibility of encountering Federal patrols with little warning, finding places to stay that were safe, and having to hide in swamps and in shacks with people Benjamin didn't know must have been a relief. But now they had to sail in open waters where they could be spotted miles away, with few places to hide from the ever-present Union Navy.

These patrols were on the lookout for any of the fleeing Confederates from Jefferson Davis's administration, as well as any military officers who might be with them. Going ashore for any reason could mean capture by some of the hundreds of Union soldiers and cavalry that were still searching on land for rebel fugitives fleeing the country.

Judah Benjamin was now traveling with one of the most knowledgeable sea captains in Florida, Frederick Tresca, who had navigated these Gulf Coast waters since he arrived at Key West as an immigrant from France in 1838. Tresca had been a successful blockade runner during the war and had made many trips to Cuba, getting trade goods out of Florida and bringing in military supplies. Hiram McLeod also has experience as a mariner and has worked with Tresca many times.

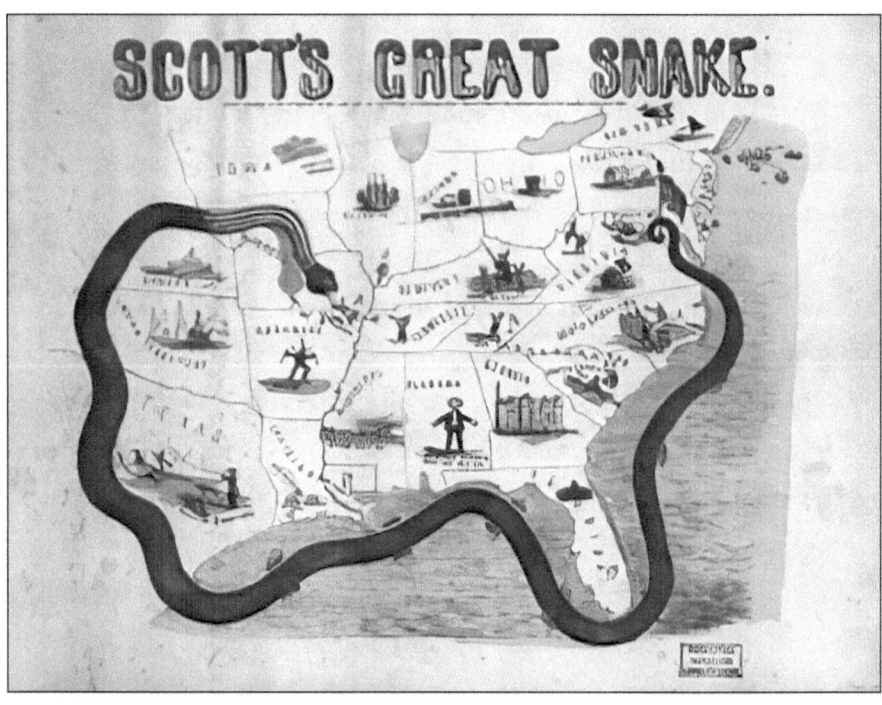

Cartoon map of Anaconda Plan

Benjamin devised a new disguise to explain his presence on this small boat. He could no longer claim to be Charles Howard, a farmer looking for land in Florida. He would now assume the role of a cook and dress the part for the eventual questioning from the Federal Navy when they were stopped. That event would happen very soon!

The three men certainly had some idea of the danger they had sailed into at this point of their trip. The Union blockade of the Confederate states, dubbed the "Anaconda Plan" by the Northern press, had a significant presence in the area. At the confluence of the Myakka and Peace Rivers, Charlotte Harbor was a major artery for blockade runners to bring cattle to the Confederate army.

Useppa Island, a scant five miles south of Gasparilla Island in Pine Island Sound, had a small Union Army and Navy encampment there since 1862. Fort Myers, only fifteen miles upriver on the Caloosahatchee River, was occupied by the Union Army and militia forces. The fort had been built during the Third Seminole War, which ended in 1858, a few years before the outbreak of the Civil War. Fort Jefferson, in the Dry Tortugas, was a primary naval site for the Union. It was a coaling station for gunboats patrolling the Gulf of Mexico and the waters north of Cuba.

This first known contact with the Navy occurred near Boca Grande, about fifty miles south of Whitaker Bayou. The group spotted a Federal gunboat as its crew was lowering a small boat into the water to chase after the fugitives. Tresca quickly turned into Gasparilla Pass and behind Gasparilla Island. The trio lowered the sail and mast and hid among the dense mangroves.

The Federals circled the island several times and passed so close to the group that they could clearly hear the sailors talking. Staying hidden for several hours, they decided it was safe to go ashore on Gasparilla Island and decided to spend a couple of days there just to be safe. They were afraid to build a cooking fire, so they ate crackers after landing on the island. At about 10:00 p.m., they felt it was safe to light a fire. They prepared a meal of coffee, fried bacon, and two redfish they had caught earlier.

This island had reputedly been the lair of the legendary Spanish pirate Jose Gaspar, who had plundered merchant ships and created terror among the sailors of the Florida coastline. Jose Gaspar may have been a mythical figure, but pirates had been active on the island. The fugitives may have been calmed by the waves crashing on the shore of the nearly deserted island, and the emerald-green waters looked like the waters they would soon encounter in the Caribbean.

But this upcoming part of the journey was fraught with the dangers of being stopped by the Union Navy, which could appear with little warning. They may have taken the time to observe the Navy ships' movements to determine how many were in the area and if there was a way through the blockade.

The three men in their small boat traveled only at night when there was open water. When barrier islands were available to hide behind, they would sail in daylight. This plan worked well for much of the trip, but there was a close call once. One night, they set sail in open waters at dusk since there was no inside passage along this coast. Once in open water, the winds died out, and they had to wait helplessly for the wind to return. By then, it was daylight, and they had been spotted by a patrol boat, which was very near and heading their way.

Tresca and McLeod had to think quickly, so they told Benjamin to lie at the bottom of the boat. They covered him with canvas, bedding, old fish nets, and dunnage. They also put water in the bottom of the hull to make it look like a person could not possibly be hiding underneath it all. This may have reminded Judah of his time in the wagon under a pile of meat and palmettos a few weeks prior. When the patrol boat came alongside, they could see it was a small and insignificant little yawl, so they did not bother sending a boarding party. Tresca and McLeod were relieved to see the patrol boat steam away towards the horizon.

Another narrow escape happened after passing present-day Sanibel and Captiva. A Federal gunboat had spotted the group and sailed towards them, intending to stop the little sailboat. Before getting too close, Benjamin donned a cook's apron and skull cap and smeared some grease on his face and clothes. The sailors boarded the boat and asked where they were headed. Tresca informed them they were fishermen working to supply some people on shore nearby. The nets and fishing tackle on board helped to confirm their story.

Still a little suspicious, one sailor stared at Benjamin as he stirred charcoal in a small sandbox they used for cooking. He remarked "that he had never seen a Jew doing common labor before." He turned away, reboarded his ship, and the gunboat finally sailed out of sight. Unfortunately for the trio, no more islands would be between them and the Federal ships in the Gulf of Mexico. They would be visible for miles in the open waters until they reached Knight's Key.

The voyagers would run low on food and water, so they occasionally went ashore to find coconuts, turtle eggs, and drinking water. They stopped at some of the fishing camps or ranchos along the coast but were careful not to reveal too much since they did not know who they could trust among the people they encountered.

At Cape Romano-Ten Thousand Islands, the group went ashore and found a stand of banana trees. They helped themselves, and Benjamin was quite fond of them. It was in this area that they encountered some large alligators as well as Seminoles[1]. The meeting of both was a cause for concern, but they safely moved through the area.

The little yawl and its crew finally made it to Cape Sable after enduring two weeks of the tropical sun and hordes of mosquitoes. The area was patrolled by many navy gunboats since this part of Florida was the last of US territory before making the open seas towards Cuba. Unknown to the three mariners, Union troops based in Key West had been sent overland to Key Biscayne and Cape Sable to watch for any escaping Confederates that might be traveling through the area.

The soldiers at Cape Sable managed to catch a few fugitives, but they were minor government officials. Shortly before Judah Benjamin and company had passed this area, the troops were ordered to return to Key West. Had they stayed there for a few more days, they might have ended Benjamin's escape plans. Somehow, the trio had managed to avoid all these hazards and turned east towards the chain of islands of the Florida Keys. They made landfall at Knight's Key and met with William Henry Bethel.

Bethel had been a fellow blockade runner during the Civil War and wrecker[2] before the war, salvaging some of the many ships that crashed on the reefs of the Florida Keys. Knights Key was sparsely populated, with only two families living there. Bethel had been a US Customs Inspector and Postmaster on Indian Key. Certainly, Tresca knew of Bethel. To cross the Gulf Stream to the Bahamas, Tresca would need a bigger boat. Bethel provided him with the sloop *Blonde*.

---

1   Most of the Seminoles had been relocated to Oklahoma by 1858, but about two hundred had hidden in the Everglades and refused to surrender. These were the ancestors of the Seminole Tribe of Florida today.

2   "Wreckers" were mariners who salvaged the cargoes of ships that had wrecked on reefs and shoals. They were able to sell the cargo for a profit.

Here, Judah Benjamin learned that there was a $50,000 bounty for his capture. The three mariners began planning to cross the Straits of Florida and make landfall somewhere in the Bahamas, and freedom!

Tresca, McLeod, and Benjamin wasted little time at Knight's Key with Bethel. However, they took time for a hearty breakfast, as it had been a while since they could enjoy good food in a pleasant setting. Tresca was unsure if he could trust Bethel because the reward money was so tempting. They set sail as soon as they could via Hawk Channel and headed into the Straits of Florida and eastward towards Bimini. Mother Nature would test the three men's sailing skills and their sloop's seaworthiness.

Chapter Twenty

Escape to Bimini and Nassau

After sailing for two days, the men noticed dark clouds forming on the horizon. It was a line of squalls, and they thought them to be far enough away that they would be safe. The heat had been intense for most of the day, and these were perfect conditions for thunderstorm formation. As the storm came closer from the west, Tresca ordered the sail to be lowered so they could ride out the wind and rain.

Soon, the cloud dipped into the water, and two large waterspouts formed and headed their way. A waterspout is a tornado that forms over water and has high winds, rain, and lightning. The largest of the two waterspouts engulfed the boat, and the men were deluged with rain and high winds. They bailed water out of the boat as fast as possible to prevent sinking. Tresca struggled to maintain some control of the small vessel, and McLeod used a bucket while Benjamin used his hat to toss water out of the boat.

After many minutes of sheer terror, the storm passed, and the winds were calm again. Judah Benjamin remarked to McLeod, with his dry wit and smile, "McLeod, this is not like being Secretary of

State." McLeod replied, "No, but you're better off here than facing the Federals."

Benjamin and company arrived at Bimini in the Bahamas on July 10, 1865, after nearly sixty hours at sea and enduring the Caribbean's sun, heat, and storms. He paid Tresca and McLeod the agreed-upon sum of $1,500 plus expenses. He sent presents back with them for their wives and bid them farewell. It was a testament to the character and loyalty of Tresca and McLeod since they could have made a lot more money by turning Benjamin over to the authorities. But they were true to their word and went on their way. But Judah Benjamin's adventures were far from over yet!

Benjamin was now on British soil and finally safe from capture by the United States government. Being born in St. Croix when it was a British possession allowed him to claim dual citizenship. However, there was not much in Bimini that would make him want to stay. He needed to get to a bigger port city where larger ships transited if he wanted to get out of the Caribbean.

Bimini had been 125 miles from Knight's Key, and Nassau, the capital city of the Bahamas, was another 125 miles away. In Nassau, his chances of finding a larger vessel going to Cuba or Great Britain were much better. Benjamin roamed the streets of Alice Town, looking for a captain who could take him to Nassau. He found a Bahamian captain, Elias Rolle, who operated a large sloop locally called *"Josephine."* Benjamin negotiated the price of passage and boarded the ship. It had a crew of three, with Judah as its one passenger, and a hold packed with wet sponges being shipped to Nassau. The *Josephine,* towing a small skiff, departed Bimini on July 11 on what should have been a routine voyage, but they would not get far!

Thirty miles out to sea on the Mackies Bank, the sloop began taking on water rapidly. The cargo of wet sponges had started drying out in the warm air and expanded and hardened. This caused the ships' sides to break apart due to the pressure. The boat sank so fast that the crew and passengers barely had time to get in the skiff and were luckily able to get a barrel of fresh water, some bananas, a pot of cooked rice, and one oar. It was better than nothing! Now, they were adrift in open waters, with nobody knowing what had happened and no way of communicating with anyone. The small boat was not intended to hold so many people, and the hull rode barely five inches above the water. They could not make much progress with only one oar and had to keep bailing water out. They could only hope that a passing ship would spot them soon before they drifted out of the regular lanes of ship traffic or sank outright.

Their luck was good, with only eight hours passing before they were spotted by the British-flagged H. M. B. Lighthouse Yacht, *Georgina*. This ship had been on an inspection tour of the Bahama's lighthouses, but its Captain, W. H Stuart, generously agreed to take the crew and passengers back to Bimini before resuming his tour.

Captain Stewart, in a report to the governor about the incident, wrote:

> "...I fell in with a small boat containing three men composing the crew of the sloop *Josephine* of Bimini, Elias Rolle master, and a gentleman passenger that stated privately to me that he is Mr. Benjamin, Secretary of State for the late Southern Confederacy, who has made his escape across the Gulf of Florida to Bimini in an open boat, whence he took passage in the above-named sloop for Nassau."

After returning to Bimini, Benjamin pondered his next move and began looking for another boat and captain to take him to Nassau. As luck would have it, his friends Frederick Tresca and Hiram

McLeod were still in Alice Town and agreed to take him to Nassau on the *Blonde*. They left Bimini on July 15 and had to endure six days of headwinds, summer thunderstorms, and the possibility of more waterspouts, calm winds, and the relentless sun. Arriving at the port of New Providence on July 21, Benjamin said he "was contented and cheerful under all reserves." However, his arrival did not go unnoticed by the American Consulate in Nassau. They notified Washington by telegram of his arrival "in a small sloop-rigged vessel called the *Blonde*. She brought him from Tampa Bay, Florida, and left him in the Biminis." Upon learning of Benjamin's successful arrival in the Bahamas, President Andrew Johnson remarked to a friend, "... there was no rebel, whose hanging seemed to him so imperatively demanded by public justice, as Judah P. Benjamin."

Judah Benjamin wasted no time in departing Nassau in a small schooner and headed for Havana, Cuba, on July 22, arriving three days later. He found a small group of ex-Confederates there and spent some time catching up on their travels and news from home. Kirby Smith, John Taylor Wood, and William Breckinridge were already in Havana. Wood and Breckinridge, whom Benjamin had last seen at Ocala, had escaped across Florida and traveled down the east coast, sailing from Jupiter Inlet and eventually arriving at Havana. Kirby Smith had arrived from Texas and then on to Vera Cruz, Mexico, thus ending Davis's hope of restarting the government in Texas had he avoided capture.

Benjamin inquired of Smith about his brother Joseph and his sister Rebecca's son Lionel, who had served in the Confederate Army. But Smith was unable to provide any new information about their fates. Benjamin was also able to locate a second cousin, Alexander Benjamin, who was the grandson of his Uncle Emmanuel and living in Havana.

While in Havana, Benjamin took the opportunity to purchase some new clothes, which he would surely need when he arrived in Great Britain. Alexander agreed to take a letter to his family in LaGrange, Georgia. In Havana, Benjamin learned that Jefferson Davis was imprisoned at Fort Monroe, Virginia.

Benjamin knew it would be unlikely for him to sail directly from Havana to England, so he sailed for St. Thomas in the British Virgin Islands on a small schooner and arrived there after a few days at sea on August 6, 1865. The trip had been uneventful, but the next leg of his journey would be anything but that.

Chapter Twenty-One

England

At St. Thomas, Benjamin booked passage on a larger ship bound for Southampton, England, a week later. On the evening of August 13, while still sixty miles from land, a fire broke out below deck and threatened to engulf the ship. Benjamin wrote of the incident afterward:

> "by dint of great exertion and admirable conduct by all on board, the flames were kept from bursting through the deck until we got back to the harbor at St. Thomas, where we arrived at about 3 o'clock in the morning with seven feet of water in the hold poured in by steam pumps, and the deck burned to one-eighth of an inch of the entire thickness."

Undeterred by this frightening turn of events, Benjamin booked passage again and departed St. Thomas on August 15 after a two-week voyage arrived at Southampton, England, on August 30, 1865, a free man! This is not the end of the story, however. Judah Benjamin would quickly reinvent himself in his newly adopted country and achieve new successes.

Benjamin did not forget the people most instrumental in his final escape. He purchased ten-yard bolts of black silk, which would have been unavailable to Southerners after the end of the war. He sent it to Louise Tresca, Frederick Tresca's wife, and Ellen, Archibald McNeill's wife, in appreciation of their help. ed.

Benjamin now needed some money to get established in his new home in London. His funding came from the one hundred bales of cotton he had placed in storage in England before the war, which should have lasted until he could get established in a new career. However, the failure of the bank holding his account caused the loss of his fortune.

He next pursued the idea of becoming a barrister, but admission to the bar of London required three years of study of the English legal system. He got assistance from Sir George Turner and Sir George Giffard, who were lord justices, Vice-Chancellor William Page Wood, and others. Benjamin was granted a dispensation from the requirement. By working as a law clerk in the office of Charles Pollock, he had access to a law library and began studying law.

Benjamin also earned income from writing a column for a daily newspaper. He was a man of fame to the elite of the city. Benjamin Disraeli, a statesman and twice prime minister, expressed a willingness to assist him however he could. Several members of the House of Commons and the House of Lords were similarly eager to help.

Jefferson Davis was released after two years of imprisonment, and all charges were dropped. None of the cabinet members or other government officials of the Confederacy were prosecuted either. The Federal government realized that the charge of treason wouldn't be sustainable since Davis hadn't advocated the overthrow of the government but had advocated secession by the Confederate States. It was also a concern by the prosecutors that it may be proven that secession was not illegal.

One exception was Captain Henry Wirz, the camp commandant of the notorious Confederate prison at Andersonville, Georgia. Wirz was tried and found guilty of conspiracy and murder because of the inhumane conditions of the camp. He was condemned to death but was offered to be spared if he would implicate Jefferson Davis as being responsible for the way the camp was run and the horrific conditions thervanishWirz refused to make false statements about Davis to save himself and was hanged by the government on November 10, 1865, the only Confederate officer executed after the war.

Benjamin's activities as a spymaster during the war would now come back to haunt him in his new home. 1867, Secretary of State William Seward sent General George Sharpe to London to track down Benjamin and capture him. Seward had been severely wounded in a knife attack by one of Booth's co-conspirators in the Lincoln assassination. For him, the capture of Benjamin was personal. Benjamin would then be returned to the United States to face charges in the plot to assassinate Lincoln.

Sharpe went to London in February 1867 and began his investigation of Benjamin. He enlisted the help of Benjamin Moran, the No. 2 diplomat in the U. S. Legation (embassy). Moran kept notes on Sharpe's activities; initially, the entries were confident that progress was being made. There were no firm plans on how Judah would be captured or how he would be gotten out of the country.

The journal entries stopped by May, and Sharpe returned to the United States. The idea of bringing Judah Benjamin back to face charges was quietly dropped.

In 1868, his old friend Jefferson Davis visited Benjamin in London to consult with him on a lawsuit he was considering against an author of a book that was unfavorable to him. Benjamin advised against it since it would likely start a war of words between the author and Davis in the newspapers. Benjamin reasoned that if Davis refused to respond or to take the author to court, the book would vanish into oblivion. Davis followed his old friend and counselor's advice, and the incident faded away.

Davis wrote a two-volume memoir of the war years titled *"The Rise and Fall of the Confederate Government,"* first published in 1881. He had consulted with Benjamin on the work but barely mentioned him in it. Jefferson Davis died on December 6, 1889, at the age of 81.

Benjamin worked tirelessly and wrote a book on the legal aspects of property sales called *"A Treatise on the Law of Sales of Personal Property,"* commonly referred to as *"Benjamin on Sales,"* which became an international reference and is still used in England today. When asked how he could be so financially successful, he replied, "First, I charge a retainer; then I charge a reminder; next, I charge a refresher; and then I charge a finisher."

In 1874, he turned his attention to his only child, Ninette, who was approaching thirty and had no marriage prospects yet. She was unlike her mother, being shy and self-effacing. Benjamin offered a dowry of $3000 per year to a suitor. Ninette had met a French Army Officer, Henri deBousignac, of whom Natalie approved and came from a socially acceptable background. Writing to a sister, he described him:

> "Captain deBousignac, her intended, is represented on all sides as one of the most promising officers of the French Army. At the age of thirty-two, he has acquired a distin-

guished position on the general staff from his merits as both an artillery and engineer officer; he is of excellent family, irreproachable habits, beloved by all around him for his frank, gay, and amiable character…He is stationed at Versailles, only half an hour from Paris, and as long as he remains there, the new couple will live with us."

Epilogue

As in New Orleans, his caseload increased, and his successes made him an acknowledged leader in the English Bar and one of the most highly paid barristers. He retired for the last time after seventeen years of practice. He was given a farewell from his many colleagues, who were the most distinguished of the English Bar. Benjamin responded with a speech of rhetorical beauty, which he had been known for in America, and with a note of sadness. He would now move to Paris to be with his wife.

Benjamin in judges' wig and robe

In 1879, he was busy supervising the construction of a mansion in Paris located at 41 Avenue d 'Jena, which cost $80,000. Natalie and Ninette busied themselves with the interior furnishings and decoration. It was his only other real home since building Belle Chasse in New Orleans years before the war.

He was seriously injured in May of 1880 when he fell from a tram car in Paris, jumping off while it was still in motion. He tore his right arm from its socket, fractured his shoulder blade, and sustained a fractured forehead. He recovered surprisingly fast and was back at work in London. But this would not last long as his injury affected his health.

Benjamin had grown tired of the workload of his law practice and was considering retirement. The decision was forced upon him at Christmas in 1882 when he suffered a severe heart attack that was brought on by many years of diabetes. He reportedly returned retainers totaling $100,000, confirming his retirement. The closing of his law practice was national news, and Benjamin received many letters from colleagues and former clients. In a letter to his sister

> "...I have hardly kept my eyes free from tears on reading these testimonials to rectitude and honor of my professional conduct, such that no member of the bar has ever received."

Benjamin now moved permanently to Paris to live with Natalie in the mansion he had built for her many years before. He would not enjoy it for long. He had requested of the executor of his estate, John George DeWitt, "Never keep any letter or any document if you can help it. You will only give yourself infinite trouble, and if you die, you bequeath a legacy of mischief."

Judah Phillip Benjamin died on May 6, 1883, and was buried in the Pere Lachaise Cemetery in Paris. It is an old cemetery in the city's heart, built on the high ground near the Seine River, and is now surrounded by high-rise apartments. Nearly all the burials are in above-ground crypts, as is Benjamin's. Maybe in a final attempt at disguise and anonymity, the name carved on the headstone is "Philippe Benjamin" which his wife Natalie called him. The Paris Chapter of the Daughters of the Confederacy added a stone in 1938 with the inscription:

Judah Philip Benjamin
Born St. Thomas West Indies August 6, 1811
Died in Paris May 6, 1884,
United States Senator from Louisiana
Attorney General, Secretary of War and
Secretary of State of the Confederate States
of America, Queens Council, London

The fates of the few Confederates who escaped the United States were each very different. John Taylor Wood, who had been with the presidential party since the fall of Richmond, eventually made his way to Cuba after traveling down the east coast of Florida along with John Breckinridge. It is a story of survival and ingenuity that rivals Judah Benjamin's escape. He left Havana, Cuba, on the former blockade runner "*Lark*" on June 23, 1865, arriving in Nova Scotia a week later. He settled in Halifax and was joined there by his wife. He began a new life working in the shipping and maritime insurance industries. He died on July 19, 1904, and is buried there in Camp Hill Cemetery.

John Breckinridge escaped to Southampton, England, on July 6, 1865, after being at sea for three weeks. On the voyage, he completed a manuscript about his wartime experiences. Leaving England, he sailed to Toronto, Canada, where he was joined by his wife and two of their children.

Breckinridge was aware that President Johnson was eager to capture him, and he was concerned about his proximity to the United

States border. There were standing orders for his arrest should he enter the United States. Breckinridge soon moved to London, where he was somewhat of a celebrity, being entertained by British royalty. He met Gladstone and the Archbishop of Canterbury and spent his time in exile enjoying the benefits of his notoriety.

President Johnson issued a general amnesty in 1868, allowing Breckenridge to return to his former home in Kentucky. There, he quietly practiced law until his premature death at age fifty-four.

General Kirby Smith, on whom Jefferson Davis had pinned his hopes of continuing the Confederacy in the Trans-Mississippi Region, first fled to Mexico after the surrender of his department eight weeks after Lee's surrender at Appomattox. He soon fled to Cuba, fearing arrest and trial for treason. He returned to the United States and took the amnesty oath on November 14, 1865, in Lynchburg, Virginia. He was involved in the telegraph business for three years before accepting the professor position at the University of the South in Sewanee, Tennessee. He taught there until his death from pneumonia in 1893. He was the last surviving general of the Civil War.

References

1. Judah Benjamin, Counselor to the Confederacy – James Traub, 2021

2. Judah P. Benjamin, Confederate Statesman – Robert Douthat Meade, 1943

3. Judah P. Benjamin, The Jewish Confederate – Eli N. Evans, 1988

4. Judah P. Benjamin, Statesman of the Lost Cause – Rollin Osterweis,1933

5. Journey to Asylum – Don Lankiewicz, 2015

6. Flight Into Oblivion – Alfred J. Hanna, 1938

7. Judah Benjamin – S. I Neiman, 1963

8. Judah P. Benjamin – Pierce Butler1906

9. Edge of Wilderness, A Settlement History of Manatee River and Sarasota Bay, 1983

10. The Rise and Fall of the Confederate Government – Jefferson Davis, 2017

11. Thundersticks, Firearms and the Violent Transformation of Native America – David J. Silverman, 2016

12. Ocali Country, Kingdom of the Sun – Eloise Robinson Ott and Louis Hickman Chazal,

13. Manatee County Historical Records Library, 1405 4th Avenue West, Bradenton, FL 34205

14. Manatee County Public Library System, 1301 Barcarotta Boulevard, Bradenton, FL, 34205

15. Sarasota County Libraries and Historical Resources, 6062 Porter Way, Sarasota, FL 34232

16. Marion County Museum of History and Archaeology, 307 SE 26th Terrace, Ocala, FL